BUILD BETTER CHARACTERS

THE PSYCHOLOGY OF BACKSTORY & HOW TO USE IT IN YOUR WRITING TO HOOK READERS

EILEEN COOK

CREATIVE ACADEMY FOR WRITERS

Published by Creative Academy for Writers for Writers

www.creativeacademyforwriters.com

Disclosure: When there are products or services we like and use ourselves, we've included an affiliate link. It's a win-win, you get something that we love and we get a small amount of money that we will blow on champagne and books.

ISBNs

978-1-926691-93-0 (Mobi)

978-1-990220-03-6 (ePub)

978-1-926691-95-4 (Softcover)

978-1-990220-02-9 (Hardcover)

978-1-926691-97-8 (Audiobook)

CONTENTS

PART V

CH-CH-CH-CHANGES

To all the writers who created characters that felt real to me.
Thank you.

A note about spelling…

All three of the founding members of The Creative Academy live in Canada, and we made a conscious decision to use Canadian spellings throughout our book series. Because…well…it's who we are, eh?!

A note to our American readers and other friends from around the world… we welcome U in Canada :) Thanks for your willingness to learn new things and play nice with your colourful Canadian neighbours!

While we always appreciate readers letting us know if you find errors in our books, pretty please double check Canadian spellings before you tell us we're wrong!

When we're quoting someone and the quote had American spellings, we left those intact.

xo Eileen, Crystal and Donna

THE PHILOSOPHY OF THE CREATIVE ACADEMY FOR WRITERS

Like most writers, I started as a reader. I would go to the library every week with my parents to check out a massive stack of books. When I realized that someone was responsible for making up those stories, I knew that was what I wanted to do. I got in the habit of running my finger down the shelves to where my future (as yet completely unwritten) book would go. Then I'd jam my hand in there and shove the books on either side over a bit to make room for me. One day there was already a space. Someone else had moved the books! The children's librarian came over and whispered, "Don't worry, I'm saving room for you."

She was one of the first people to believe in my dream of being a writer....

Writers need someone to believe in our dream to help hold us up during the times when we feel like letting go. Choosing to write takes courage. Courage to continue to try during the times when the words won't come. Courage to share your work with others and invite their feedback. Courage to send it off into the world, be that through agents and editors or by indie publishing your story. The bad news is that the world has too many people who will tell you that dream is foolish and instead of encouraging, will go out of their way to discourage you. It's easier to tear down someone else's dream than it is to work toward one of your own. What you need to do is surround yourself with the *right* people.

That's why we started The Creative Academy for Writers. We wanted to create an inclusive place that fostered big dreams for writers and provided practical guidance to reach those dreams. We wanted to build a community of like-minded people, offer encouragement and practical support, and assist people in taking the next steps on their writing journey. We wanted to be that voice in your ear that says "you got this" when you feel like you very much don't.

This book is hopefully a part of that journey for you and if you aren't already, we hope you'll consider joining us online at The Creative Academy—a community is always stronger when it grows to include great people. And don't worry—we're making some space on the shelves for you. There's always room.

HOW TO GET THE MOST FROM THIS BOOK

I'm one of those people who dislikes clutter. Put me in a crowded space and I get antsy. The exception is craft books. I could be a writing craft book hoarder. (Although there's no mummified cat under the pile—at least to my knowledge.) When we wrote this book, the goal was to combine useful information that would get you thinking about your own project, but also prompts that would jump-start your creativity.

This book is designed to be read from start to finish, but we're not going to put you in a corner if you prefer to dip in and out of things based on your interest or what sparks your creativity. Be aware the content does build on previous sections, but you don't have to have read everything to understand any one part of the book.

You'll see that all the sections have content and a checklist of things to follow up on or prompts to try out—these are called **Your Turn** sections, and the idea is to get you thinking about your manuscript.

Some prompts will get your pen moving or your keyboard clacking, but others may fall flat for you. That's fine! We've done our best to provide a lot of possible jumping off points so use the ones that spark your interest. Be aware that certain ideas or prompts will work better with some projects versus others. When in doubt, just get through that draft. If you need a little help to get that first draft written, check out the first book in this series—*Scrappy Rough Draft: Use science to strategically motivate yourself & finish writing your book* by Donna Barker, to help you get that idea out of your head and onto the page.

PART I

INTRODUCTION

1

HOW COUNSELLING LED ME TO UNDERSTAND CHARACTER

I grew up with very practical parents. While they supported my plan of becoming a writer, they also wisely advised that I should have a way to support myself. Given that I'm a big fan of things like eating and shelter, I had to agree. When I reviewed my skills, I realized I was that person other people always went to when they had a question or problem, so counselling seemed a reasonable occupational option. I liked people and suspected I would enjoy the opportunity to help others. (It also helped that counselling wouldn't require a lot of math which I hated with the white-hot passion of a thousand suns.) I went on to pursue a master's degree specializing in rehabilitation counselling where I worked with people with catastrophic injuries or illness.

Counselling provided me with the opportunity to study human behaviour. I discovered writers can learn a lot from counsellors that would help us create better characters.

These characters have more realistic responses to conflict and crisis to make our books richer and deeper. Any mistakes I made in this book are on me.

I'm going to share these character creation ideas with you. It's like a crash course in understanding people, without the worry there will be a pop quiz.

2

WHAT CAN WRITERS LEARN FROM COUNSELLORS?

Non-judgmental approach

Counsellors are trained to approach people with an open and empathetic response. It doesn't mean that the counsellor doesn't have a personal opinion about whatever the individual may be struggling with. Instead it means that when working with them we maintain a balanced approach. The goal of counselling is, of course, to assist people, not judge them.

What does this mean for writers?

It means remembering that all people are making the best choice in the moment with the knowledge and ability that they have. This doesn't mean that it's a good choice (Lord knows some people and some characters make really questionable decisions), only that they're doing the best they can. As the author or creator, you need to have empathy and understanding for what your characters are doing if you want readers to connect with those characters.

Your main character and the supporting cast will be under pressure in the book. You may be killing off people who are important to them, burning down their business or crashing an asteroid into their planet. When people are under stress, they don't always respond in the best way. If you know the core of who your characters are it will be easier to understand how they will react in different circumstances. This helps the reader understand how the character's goals and motivations are moving them forward in the story.

The villains in your story have their own goals and motivations. In many cases, they don't even know they're the bad guy—as far as they're concerned, they're the hero. When writing your antagonist, steer away from easy answers—that they're doing something bad because they're just bad people, or worse, that they're doing something bad because you need them to for the purpose of the plot. Even someone who is a sociopath has their own code of behaviour. They may not have empathy for other people, because that's the way their brain works—or doesn't work. But typically, it's not simply a desire to be mean for the sake of being mean.

Listen to what is said

Counselling is fundamentally the art of listening. Often in human interaction we're thinking of what we're going to say in response before the person has even finished speaking. It's common to interrupt with what we know is excellent advice or to fill in a blank for someone. Counselling puts this natural tendency on pause and instead allows for silences. In fact, one of the first things you learn in a counselling program is to not always respond. Often if you're quiet the other person will continue to talk. Counselling means truly attending to what the other individual is saying and the words they choose to express themselves.

What does this mean for writers?

Don't rush to shove words into your characters' mouths. Think about what they want to communicate and the words they'd choose to express themselves. This word choice is likely impacted by both their level of education (ambulate versus walk, periwinkle versus blue) and also their emotion (annoyance versus rage). We're writers; if there's anything we should know it's that words matter. Think about what words your character would choose and how their audience and their situation impact that communication.

For example, if your character is lying to someone they care about (let's assume for a good reason) how do they speak? Does their partner notice something is off?

Listen to what is not said

Counsellors pay attention not only to what the client says, but also to what *isn't* said. While we hope that everyone is aware and has insight into their own motivations and beliefs, the reality is that most of us are still working that out. (No wonder there is so much job security in counselling!)

Individuals may not know what they feel or how to best express it. For example, if I ask a client about their relationship with their mother and they respond with "My mom is such a strong woman, she's a pillar in our community." They haven't answered the question. As a counsellor, it twinges my antennae. There may be more to that relationship that the client doesn't yet know or is not yet ready to explore.

Counsellors are skilled at reading non-verbal behaviour. Does the individual lean forward or back when talking? Are their arms crossed over their chest? Jaw clenched? Picking at their fingernails?

Counsellors are looking at how a client's actions can tell them more about what may be going on inside that person. We want to know if their actions match what we expect given what they're saying, or if it seems to be a contrast. For example, if a person tells me that they're really excited to start a new job, but they're chewing on their fingernails like ears of corn dipped in butter, I know something is up. I may have to dig deeper to understand exactly what it means, but it's a signal. It could be they are taking the job because a partner really wants them to pursue that field. Or, it could be they are nervous they're not up to the task. Or, it could mean what they really want to do is an occupation they worry others will think is unacceptable. (Like writing, where you play with your imaginary friends all day.) Part of being a counsellor is digging into that possible contradiction.

What does this mean for writers?

In filmmaking, some dialogue is referred to as "on the nose." This term is used to point out conversation in which the spoken words are *exactly* what the character is thinking or feeling. It feels *off* to the listener because it's too honest for the situation. Most of us aren't that honest in our communication. Screenwriters understand that people often don't say what they think and feel.

As a writer, you may also have your characters being too in touch with what they think and feel. Readers enjoy being a part of the storytelling process. When you provide them with bread crumbs or clues, they're able to unravel the complexities of your story with you. For example, if you have this in your manuscript: *"Why John, I would love nothing more than to go out with you tonight," Kelly said, twisting the rings on her fingers.* As a reader, I see that ring twisting as telling. It makes me think that perhaps she's not quite as excited about this date as she seems to be implying, that she might be nervous or have a secret that she's keeping from John. Raising those questions, and intriguing the reader, is precisely what keeps them turning pages! Pay as much attention to what your characters don't say, and the body language they use, as to what comes out of their mouth.

Be curious about human behaviour

Fundamentally counsellors are intrigued with other people and their actions and how to assist people with the challenges they face. There is an ever-growing base of information on what motivates people, and how people respond to anything from having alcoholic parents, to surviving trauma. Counsellors are typically required to do continuing education to maintain their credentials. They are constantly learning, and the field continually adds to the body of research that already exists. What we know about how, and why, people respond in different situations, and with different backgrounds, continues to grow.

What does this mean for writers?

If you've been looking only in writing craft books for advice on how to deepen your characters or to make them more realistic, then you're missing a huge section of your library or local bookstore. Prepare to get excited about all the information that is out there for you!

The self-help section is a treasure trove of character details. Consider the issues your character may have from past addiction, PTSD, loving too much (or too little), struggling with a difficult child—I guarantee there's a book that explores this in detail. Many of these books contain case studies and examples that may spark your imagination. They also typically include suggestions for how an individual might cope better with whatever challenge they're facing.

These exercises or suggestions may provide you with a road map of how your character is going to move through those changes. For example, if you're working with a character who is dealing with addiction, there are ample books that outline what motivates people to recovery, the common pitfalls and challenges during recovery, how recovery can impact relationships, and how people cope with relapse.

For a writer it's setting up all the stages you might want to consider for your character along with believable and researched responses. If you aren't sure what book to read do a quick Google search of self-help books for the topic/area that your character is struggling with and then look at which books are rated the highest. Then be prepared for your librarian or bookseller to look at you with a different perspective after they see everything you're checking out.

The belief that people can change

Counsellors are optimists. They believe that people can and do make changes in their lives—especially when they're committed to those changes. However, counsellors also understand that change is difficult. Most individuals don't change, because it's much easier to stay in our current patterns. If you doubt this, look at how many people express a desire to eat better and increase their fitness. In the vast majority of cases, it's not a lack of information that keeps them from success. People know what they should be doing to reach that goal.

So why aren't we all hitting that ten thousand steps a day goal, with a passion for Brussels sprouts? Because it is easier to sleep a bit later than to go to the gym. And I don't care if you have a recipe for the most amazing sprouts ever—a really great cookie will taste better. (And before you get angry at my bias against the green things, I'm learning to love the humble sprout. Feel free to send me recipes.) Changing and then committing to that change is difficult.

What does this mean for writers?

Your character likely needs to make a change over the course of the book as they reach for their goal or desire in the story. They may need to learn to be a part of a team, or to trust others, or to believe in themselves. Are you making it difficult for them to make that change? Do they try and fail? We'll be talking about how people do this in more detail in the **Stages of Change** section of this book.

Psychology can teach us a lot about character motivation and reaction. In this book, we focus on backstory and the impact of that on personality and change. You'll learn how to understand where your character is coming from, and how those past experiences shaped who they are at the start of your story. It will assist you in knowing why they may make specific choices and in what areas they may be more vulnerable.

Armed with this knowledge, your characters will feel more three dimensional on the page. Readers may love or hate specific characters in your story—but they will believe in them and will be compelled to turn the pages to see how they respond next.

Ready to make that happen? Let's get started!

Your Turn

Exploring your own beliefs can be useful. Below is a checklist about people and their behaviours. Indicate true or false for each statement. There isn't a right or wrong answer to these questions (although feel free to debate it among your friends or family), rather it's part of your perspective on the world and how people move around in it. If you find yourself struggling with an answer remember that you are trying to answer it "more often than not" versus as an absolute, as there are always different situations and extenuating circumstances.

Then re-do the checklist below considering how your main character would answer those questions. You can answer the questions in your journal or notes document or download a printable character belief sheet from our **creativeacademyforwriters.com/resources** page.

True or False:

1. Most people in the world are generally good.
2. The world is random, there is no such thing as fate or destiny, things just happen.
3. Hard work is essential.
4. I'm anxious and worried about the future.
5. Common sense is not very common.
6. I have a balance of good and negative traits, but

overall, I believe that I am special and unique in this world and have something to offer.

7. If someone is kind to you, they likely want something.
8. People can, and do, change.
9. It matters a lot to me what others think of me.
10. The way to move through life successfully is to make plans, evaluate options and then choose a direction.
11. I believe that things will generally work out for the best.
12. People will take advantage of you if they have an opportunity.
13. There is some kind of "purpose" to our lives, be it religion or the universe or the great spirit—there is some source of divine energy that looks out for us.
14. Everything happens for a reason. Even in bad times, there will be something for you to learn.
15. I put myself first.
16. People are who they are, they are unlikely to ever change.
17. Life should be lived in the moment. You have to react - people who try to plan everything are missing opportunities.
18. Family and friends are my most important priority.
19. I am not concerned with what other people think of me, it is more important that I approve of what I'm doing.
20. There is no such thing as a god, mystical power or caring universe. There is the world we have here, and what we do in it is all that matters.

21. I do not feel lucky, gifted or special.

Remember there is no right or wrong with the answers above. The quiz is designed to help you begin to understand your own perspective and feelings about yourself and how you interact with the world.

3

FOUNDATION FOR CHARACTER NEEDS AND MOTIVATIONS—MASLOW'S HIERARCHY OF NEEDS

They always say that the best place to start a journey is at the beginning. A good foundation for understanding individuals and where they come from is Maslow's Hierarchy of Needs. I can hear a few of you groaning that you've heard about this theory a million times. Anyone who has taken a psychology class has likely bumped into this concept before, but stick with me, it's well worth another look—especially for writers. The Hierarchy is based on what motivates individuals and is most commonly shown as a pyramid with the base needs at the bottom and moving up from there. (See diagram below)

Maslow started with the concept that people are motivated to achieve various needs and that some of those needs take precedence over others. That your base needs must be met first, but once those are in place you will start looking around for the next level. You can imagine yourself scaling the giant pyramid, looking to be a more evolved person at every step along the way.

Psychologists point out that this isn't a direct linear path—you'll bop around between the different levels, and much like many things in life, things can be flexible depending on circumstances and/or the specific individual. So instead of scaling up that pyramid, you're far more likely to take one step forward, a step back, a step to the side and then back up again. While it's a nice idea to see yourself evolving in a nice tidy linear progression, for most of us it's not that clear.

Lastly, it's also good to remember that people can be motivated by more than one thing at a time. Maslow's Hierarchy is described as if a person would be at only one step at a time, and while there will be a base/focus where the individual sits, they may also have a foot on a different step.

Let's break down the five levels, starting at the bottom:

Physiological Needs

These are the things that you need to sustain life: air, food, shelter, clothing, etc. If these needs aren't being met you've got some big problems. People are highly motivated to make sure they have these things. People who are trained to be lifeguards are warned that a drowning person will crawl up their body and shove them underwater to get their head free and breathe. It isn't that the person they're saving doesn't appreciate what the lifeguard is trying to do for them, but the survival urge will kick in and they will shove anyone out of the way to get what they need—in this case oxygen.

What does this mean for writers?

If you have your character in life or death circumstances (i.e. they've been in a plane crash and are alone in a wind-swept remote portion of the Yukon miles from civilization with only torn clothing, a broken arm, a packet of a peanuts, and a group of bears starting to sniff around the crash site looking for a snack) their focus *must* be on survival.

In some manuscripts I've seen a character being shot at and then the writer goes on to a lovely description from the character's POV of how the broken glass looks as it rains down, the light refracting through it creating millions of tiny rainbows. Um. No. Great description, great words, but now isn't the time. If your character is being shot at or chased by bears, all they will be considering is how to get through that moment. If they are thinking about rainbows the reader is likely starting to cheer for the bear.

Threatening your character's survival needs will engage readers because the stakes are literally life or death.

Safety Needs

Once an individual has ensured that they aren't going to perish in the next moment, their focus will turn to safety. Safety concerns still have an element of life or death to them, but they are less immediate. Examples include: protection from the elements, security, order, stability and a basic freedom to live without fear.

What does this mean for writers?

These needs are common in all types of manuscripts. There may not be an immediate survival need, but there are risks. If your character is hunting down a serial killer, living in a refugee camp in space, or dealing with a regime overthrow in a historical novel, they are struggling with safety needs.

People are creatures of routine. We like to know what to expect. When we don't, we can feel uneasy or unsafe. In fiction, we're often upending a character's life, and even what might not be a life or death situation may *feel* like one to them. Explore and consider what your character needs to feel safe and secure.

Love and Belonging

Once the first two levels of needs have been met people turn to the desire to have a social connection to the world around them. This doesn't have to be romantic love, although it can include it. It's the opportunity to have one (or more) people in your life who can provide friendship, trust, and a give and take of emotion. People enjoy being part of a group, and you've likely heard the term: "I found my people."

Have you ever had the experience of walking into a space with a large group of strangers, perhaps at a conference or a party, and you start looking around trying to identify people to align with? *Whew! There's someone wearing a Harry Potter t-shirt. Clearly, we have that in common, I'm going to go stand over by them.* Conversely, if you enter the same space and everyone else seems to have gotten the memo to dress *way up* (i.e. wearing clothes that require foundational undergarments) and you haven't been out of yoga pants in five years, you'll have a different reaction. *Uh-oh, I don't belong here.*

What does this mean for writers?

There are entire genres of books that are built on a character's search for love and belonging. They will do what they can to reach out and find the person or people who will let them finally feel that they belong. This doesn't mean that they won't be independent, instead that they want to be a part of, and contribute to, a larger group—even if that group is only one special person. We all want to be loved.

As a writer ask yourself who are your character's "people?" What clues or signals would make them feel a sense of relief and welcome? What would make them feel like a fish out of water? How would they know they didn't fit in?

Esteem Needs

Maslow put these needs into two sub-sections. The first is esteem for oneself which includes dignity, achievement, mastery and independence. This also includes feeling that you like yourself, that you feel good about what you can do, and while you know you have areas to work on, overall, you're an independent functioning person. The second section is outwardly focused and includes the desire for other people to know that you've got your act together, and things like reputation and respect.

Younger people are often more concerned about having a good reputation and the respect of their peers than they are about their own opinion of themselves. If you ever succumbed to peer pressure and wore some ridiculous hairstyle because everyone else was doing it and you wanted to appear cool, this is a demonstration of that. I spent my teen years in the late '80s and I have photographic proof that I clearly had zero idea of what looked good on me. (Did asymmetrical hair look good on anyone other than band members from Flock of Seagulls?)

What does this mean for writers?

You need to know what would make your character feel good about themselves. Is there a milestone that they need to achieve? This could be anything from having a baby to getting a particular job to moving out on their own. These milestones are often visible ways of demonstrating to ourselves that we have "arrived," that we have reached the expectations we have of ourselves. What do your characters like about themselves?

How important is their reputation to them? It can be interesting to compare what the character assumes versus what other characters actually think of them. Do they feel their reputation is deserved? Accurate? For example, you may have a character who has a reputation for being really successful, but the individual may feel it's all a sham and only a matter of time before everyone finds out they don't really have it together at all. (Ah, the dreaded imposter syndrome.) Conversely, a character might have the reputation that they're a slut, but they know that the reputation is based on a lie. (Not to mention outdated and misogynistic.)

Self-Actualization

This is the top of the pyramid! Once you've addressed all the other needs, you're ready to tackle the one that can often be the most difficult. Things that are included in this section: realizing your personal potential, feeling self-fulfilled and as Maslow described the desire: "to become everything one is capable of becoming." No pressure or anything, just be all you can be.

There's a reason you see people in their fifties asking themselves some hard questions. Usually, at this point, most of their base needs have been met. They have homes, relationships, often a career that has been successful, and then they start to wonder: *Is this it?* They wonder what else they might be capable of doing. Cue the mid-life crisis in all its glory.

At this stage of life, people become aware that time isn't infinite and we begin to wonder if we should take up yoga, travel more, or write that novel. (My suggestion is go on the trip, use it as inspiration for writing a book, and take occasional stretching breaks so you don't get all hunched over.)

What does this mean for writers?

Depending on the genre, and the story you're telling, your character may be struggling with this level of need. Unlike the survival needs at the base of the pyramid that lend themselves well to high action and a fast plot, stories looking at this need tend to be more character-driven and internal. Nothing is blowing up, on fire, or shooting at you. This stage—and therefore this type of story—is about figuring out who you truly want to be.

Your Turn

- If your character is in physical danger, what is their most pressing safety concern? What scares them the most about this? How can you show that desperate need for survival?
- If your character is in a life or death situation, what might they do to survive that they wouldn't do in any other circumstance?
- If you have a situation that isn't life or death, does it feel that way to the character? What do they think they will lose if they're not successful?
- Are there relationships missing in your character's life? Are their current relationships healthy?
- Have your character do a journal entry about love. What does it mean to them? Do they feel loved?
- What would make your character feel good about themselves?
- What would your character need to do to feel successful?
- What is your character's reputation? Do they like it, are they proud of it? What would they like their reputation to be?
- If all of your character's base needs have been met, what do they need to fully become their best self?
- Write a journal entry from the POV of one of your characters where they talk about their biggest dreams. If they could do anything/be anything, what would it be?

PART II

BACKSTORY BASICS

4

WHY COUNSELLORS TAKE A BACKSTORY AS A PART OF COUNSELLING

When a counsellor meets a client for the first time they will do some type of a clinical interview. This provides an opportunity for them to collect key details about that individual's history in a range of areas before starting the counselling process. In writing terms, we call that a backstory.

Knowing where someone is coming from, their experiences, and more importantly, their beliefs about those experiences, is the foundation to understanding how to help someone move forward. Who we are and our personality is formed in part by the things that happen to us. Theorists like Freud and Skinner based significant portions of their theories on how childhood impacts us as adults.

The Nature Versus Nurture debate has been going on since we first started to explore human behaviour. While there will always be some amount of disagreement, most people concur that there's a part of our personality that is hard-wired into us. However, a significant portion of how an individual navigates the world and copes with challenges is likely due to nurture, to a set of behaviours and coping strategies built, developed, and reinforced, over time.

People tell themselves stories that help them make sense of things in the world. We all have "mythologies" about ourselves and it can be very difficult when those myths are challenged. We have a tendency to notice and pay attention to information that reinforces our existing myths and ignore information that doesn't.

For example:

> *Desmond came from a traditional family and served for a long time in the military before getting a job as a police officer. He views himself as a bit of a hero. He's strong, capable and will make sure people are safe. Desmond partly defines his concept of being a man as one who is able to provide for his wife and family.*
>
> *Then he's in a car accident and is unable to return to work. Suddenly Desmond isn't the guy at the gym who's bench pressing 300 lbs. And, where once new recruits were always assigned to him and he was looked up to at work, he's now on disability leave. His wife is working full-time, and his disability income isn't enough to cover everything. His son has had to take over doing the yard work and other heavy chores because it's too difficult for Desmond.*

Even though Desmond has survived the accident and is fundamentally the same person, his concept of who he is, and what it means to be successful, have been significantly altered. He and his spouse are likely to have challenges as they navigate new roles with one another.

Another example:

> *Luna has always seen herself as a creative person who paints, does fibre arts and is planning to write a book soon. Then she has a child, and that baby is all-consuming. She doesn't have time to write (or paint—hell, who is she kidding, she's barely had a shower in days) and while people used to call her by her name, now everyone says things like: "How's the new mommy?" She used to catch a glimpse of herself in the mirror and think: "Oooh, I'm sexy." Now her boobs are leaking all the time, there are dark circles under her eyes, and if she laughs, she pees herself a little.*

While Luna wanted a child and is glad she's a mom, she's also having to redefine herself. (And buy undergarments that prevent leakage.)

Exploring a client's history and the meaning they put onto events in their past is what allows the counsellor to begin to see the world in the present time from that individual's perspective.

The realization that not everyone sees the world as you do can be a real eye-opener. Counsellors know that in order to assist a client to see the world differently they must first be sure they know where the individual is coming from—so they take a history.

5

WHY TAKING A HISTORY (BACKSTORY) IS IMPORTANT TO WRITERS

Unless your character was born on page one of your manuscript, they come to the start of the book with a history, a backstory. They've had things happen to them, and have developed feelings about those events, other people, and themselves, as a result.

Taking the time to understand where your character comes from will help you deepen your point of view (POV) and emotion on the page. While you won't be including all of that backstory in your novel, the fact that you know it will shape how you write those characters. Readers will feel that they truly "know" that person, and while they may or may not like them, they will understand them.

A character's history shapes the decisions they make throughout the novel and will make their motivation clearer to the reader, including why they may make bad decisions or continue to try even under difficult circumstances. As you and your character face a new fork in the road, you'll find it easier to know which direction they'll travel. And if you stumble into a situation where you need a character to decide to do X, but their backstory clearly indicates that they would do Y, you'll have your own decision to make—either changing their backstory or changing their response. This will save you from having to do a more substantial revision later when things "just don't feel right."

Fundamentally, writing is about putting characters in extraordinary circumstances. As writers, we're often not very nice to our imaginary friends. We throw everything at them from asteroids to goblins to disastrous relationships. The study of human behaviour tells us that under pressure, we revert to our core beliefs and are increasingly vulnerable when our buttons are pushed and we're reacting. It's essential that you understand what those core beliefs are so that whatever thin veneer of coping the character has managed to create in their world cracks when you up the pressure on the page, and you know exactly how they'll respond.

We've spoken so far about how an individual's beliefs shape their own reactions and decisions, but the cliché tells us—no man is an island. That means that our beliefs also impact how we react to other people's actions and decisions. If someone we interact with has an opposing world view, there's going to be conflict. And there is nothing that should make a writer's heart go pitter-pat more than the opportunity for increasing conflict on the page.

You've likely seen this in your own life. If you're someone who believes that being spontaneous is what makes life fun, then on vacation you might like to drive until the spirit tells you to pull over and explore. What if you're travelling with a person who has mapped out the entire road trip complete with suggestions for when and where to take bathroom breaks and has a tidy binder of all the roadside attractions (Including notes on if there are fees to get in and the opening and closing hours)? It's going to be a rough trip. There are entire movies and stories based strictly on this theme of being an "odd couple"—two people with very different perspectives who are forced to interact.

Consider how different characters view the world. You can use the quiz in **Chapter 2: What can writers learn from counsellors?** to generate some ideas about perspectives. Rather than having two of your characters in your book see the world in the same way, play with having them on different ends of the spectrum.

For example, if I believe that the world is a cold and cruel place where everyone is out to get me and I meet someone who believes the world is fundamentally a good place and that most people will help you as needed, we're going to butt heads. Or play with the idea that two characters share the same worldview (again that the world is a hard and cruel place) and then one of the characters begins to change. That change is going to push the other. It's going to impact how they interact and get along.

A key thing to remember is that characters don't always have accurate insight. Real people often don't know why they do things. Their reactions may happen on an instinctive level, knee jerk, so to speak. There is also the possibility that the individual will tell themselves a story about why they do something that may not be the truth but instead supports their mythology.

Example:

> *Cathy's had a difficult childhood. Her mother was an addict and her father tried to keep it covered up so that others wouldn't know because he worried about what people would think. Her life had a lot of instability as a result. Now as an adult she's very focused on her success. She looks down on people who don't wear the right brands of clothing, drive the right car, or eat at the right restaurants.*

She might describe herself as being selective and not be aware that she feels status items are required for approval, and that having expensive things is her way to feel safe and secure.

Areas of backstory

The contents of a clinical interview vary from counsellor to counsellor and also depend on the setting the counsellor works in and the goals of counselling. The following sections are broken out into areas that may be touched on in an interview and why a counsellor may ask those questions. You'll see the questions framed as if a counsellor was asking them to an individual.

You can download the entire interview as a printable worksheet from our **https://creativeacademyforwriters.com/resources/buildbettercharacters/** page.

FAMILY AND SOCIAL SUPPORT

Examples of questions that fall into this area of a counselling interview:

- What were your parents like?
- Do you have any siblings?
- Where are you in the birth order of your family? (Oldest child, only child, baby of the family)
- Did you get along with your parents? With your family?

Why this information is important

As we discussed earlier, there's an ongoing debate between nurture and nature, but there's no confusion among mental health therapists that events during our early childhood are vitally important.

Identity formation happens over a period of time. The messages we get from our family imprint on our young brains. Children who get messages that they are loved, safe, or that they have value, typically go on to have an easier time developing healthy adult relationships and self-regard. Children who have difficult early years may imprint messages like, "I don't deserve love." As a result, they may unconsciously seek out relationships where they are poorly treated as it reinforces what they already believe to be true.

If you've spent any time on social media, you'll eventually see a meme about birth order that highlights how either the youngest child is always the best-looking or the eldest is the smartest. (And let's give a call out to us only children who are clearly the most well-adjusted.) Siblings have been fighting over what is the best place to be for generations and the only agreement seems to be that being the middle child is the hardest.

Firstborn children often have more of their parent's attention and focus than next-born children and as a result can be more independent. They tend to be "mini-adults" who are reliable, structured, controlling and high-achieving. Their age before the rest of their siblings enter the picture will make a difference. Once brothers and sisters show up, firstborns often take on some of the caregiving responsibility.

Middle children have the difficulty of looking for their role. They're not the baby and they're not the oldest. They may feel they get the least amount of their parent's attention. Middle children are often described as thriving on friendships, possibly rebellious, and often taking on the role of the peacemaker.

The baby of the family typically has the benefit of the most relaxed parents. They may be doted on by both parents and older siblings. They're often described as fun-loving, out-going, may be self-centred and skilled at negotiating to get what they want.

Counsellors are also keen to know if a client's family is still a possible source of social support. Does the individual have parents, siblings, children, cousins, etc. that they can call upon? If your character does have a strong support network this will often be their go-to place for help. You may have to consider if you need to get rid of their family in some way if you need the character to stand on their own. (Only writers would callously discuss the need to kill off some family members for our plot needs. Well, us and serial killers.)

Your Turn

- Create a family tree / relationship tree or journal entry where your character talks about an early childhood memory.
- Your character's conflicts with their family members are a possible source of interesting backstory. What led up to this division? Is it something that should (or could) be healed over the course of the story, or is it a relationship best left separate?

- One way to think about a character's memories and their impact—is to think about your own, noticing what sticks out to you and what you might take from that in terms of how you view the world. In essence, I'm asking you to be your own counsellor.
- List the first memory of your own childhood that comes to mind and then 2-3 more.
- For each memory write out as much as you can recall about it. Sights, smells, sounds and what happened.
- Now how would you interpret this memory if you were a counsellor? Why do you think it stands out for you? What meaning might you put on to that memory? How has that situation/event impacted you later in life?
- Do you ever wonder if your memories are accurate? Do you have a childhood memory of an event or experience that a sibling has a *completely* different memory of?

RACE AND CULTURE

Examples of questions that fall into this area of a counselling interview:

- What is your ethnic background?
- What role (if any) does your culture play in your life?
- Are there cultural traditions that are important to you?
- What would your cultural background say about the situation you're currently in?

If an individual is an immigrant, questions may include:

- When did you immigrate to this country?
- Did you immigrate on your own or with a family group?

- What circumstances led up to your decision to immigrate?
- How do you feel about your new country?

Why this information is important

Our racial and cultural backgrounds influence not only how we see ourselves, but also how others view us. For some people, their background provides both a sense and the reality of privilege. For others it's the opposite. For some individuals, race and culture is a huge source of pride and a defining characteristic. Not so for another group. As a society, we're still exploring what those things mean and how bias may impact our interactions and societal structures.

Individuals who are immigrants face unique challenges in determining what part of their culture and history will remain a focus and how they will integrate with potentially very different expectations in their new country. It's also important to understand that if an individual had to immigrate due to war or natural disaster, they might be coping with additional trauma on top of any other issues they are working through.

There are entire books, workshops, and important online discussions happening on the issue of writing characters who might be outside of your own background. Take time to educate yourself on this topic and the importance of marginalized voices being heard. There's value in ensuring that your world is reflective of the real world and thus is likely populated by people from a wide range of backgrounds.

However, it is also essential that if you're writing outside of your personal experience that you get those details right and don't fall into clichés or get things wrong and move forward incorrect (and painful) stereotypes. Yes, people are people, and we all have similar struggles and challenges, but those experiences are filtered and impacted by things like culture and race.

Your Turn

- If your character has a racial, cultural or religious background different than your own, what research have you done to get those details right?
- Can you identify anyone with a similar background who you could speak to?

SOCIOECONOMIC CLASS

Examples of questions that fall into this area of a counselling interview:

- How would you describe your family's financial status as a kid?
- How is your current financial situation?
- Do you have any debt?
- What is your relationship with money?
- Would you describe yourself as a saver or a spender?
- Has that changed over your life?

Why this information is important

Our relationship to class and money is a complicated one. This can also vary from culture to culture, with some putting more emphasis on class and money than others. Even separate from how we may view ourselves, as compared to others in our society, there are some practical implications. A lack of money to ensure the basics taps into Maslow's Hierarchy of needs at that base level of security and safety. If we are unsure if we can secure food or housing, that will drive our behaviour.

Debt can cause stress, although individual reactions to debt and tolerance for being in debt do vary. Some people become stressed when they're a few hundred dollars behind. Other may become hundreds of thousands of dollars in debt before it begins to cause them stress. As a result, a counsellor is interested not only if there is debt, but the individual's comfort level with that debt. Several psychological studies have examined the impact of debt on depression, anxiety, resentment in relationships, denial, stress, and anger and frustration. Your character's struggles with debt will have an impact on how they interact with others and how they respond in unrelated situations.

If your character has wealth, they have resources. Money may not buy happiness, but it can buy distraction from being unhappy. A character with funds can purchase things that may assist them in getting what they want, a character who doesn't have funds will have to get these supports in another way. If your character has resources and funds, they can approach problems and challenges in different ways. A character with limited resources means that you as the writer are going to have to brainstorm realistic ways for them to obtain what they need.

Money can also be a source of division. Perhaps you don't have the funds to participate in activities. You're the university student on scholarship so you can't afford to join your friends on the big spring break trip. Or your problem may be the opposite because you have funds and it isolates you—no one wants to hear how you went to the south of France on your spring break when they slept nine to a room at a Best Western in Coral Gables Florida and someone threw up in the bathtub.

Your Turn

- What is your character's current financial situation?
- Are they stressed about money?
- What types of resources do they have, or lack, as a result?

MARRIAGE AND LONG-TERM RELATIONSHIPS

Examples of questions that fall into this area of a counselling interview:

- Are you currently married or in a long-term relationship?
- Have you ever been married (if yes, how did that relationship end?)
- If you've had a series of relationships, how have these begun or ended?
- Are you gay, straight, bisexual or pansexual? Are you transgender?

Why this information is important

As a society, we still have expectations that people will pair up, traditionally in a married relationship, but also as long-term couples. A lot of social energy is spent watching celebrities' pair up, separate and then pair up with someone new. There are entire magazines and websites dedicated to this topic. Some of us still may have strong feelings on the whole Brad and Angelina situation. (Any team Jen out there?) Individuals are interested in what draws people together out of curiosity, but also to help us understand our own relationships.

Counsellors are interested in patterns of loving relationships. Are they long-term? When did the couple get together and what brought them there? How do they manage conflict? Believe it or not, one warning sign is a couple that tells you they never fight. It's impossible to avoid conflict in a relationship over the long-term. A couple that doesn't fight means they don't address conflict, and that might come back to bite them.

Counsellors will ask about highs and lows in a relationship and look at how the individual tells those stories. They want to know if this is a long-term stable relationship that supports the person in growing and learning, or if it's toxic and stunting the individual from doing what they could.

An individual's sexual orientation may also be important. Is the individual happy and confident in this orientation or is this something that they've struggled with? There may be conflict when family rejects an individual's orientation so they may feel they have to choose between their family and their desire to be in a loving relationship. Again, it's important to understand that no one orientation is better than another—what's important is how that orientation impacts the individual and how they see the world.

Counsellors are also interested if these are short-term relationships. If people have had a series of relationships, none of them lasting, are there any similarities? Does the person always initiate the break-up? Are they the one who is always dumped? Do they choose a similar type of people to have relationships with? Are they learning and growing as they go from one relationship to another, or are they repeating unhealthy behaviours?

And there's also a group of people who identify as not having any interest in sexual or romantic relationships. This may be due to a difficult break-up, where the individual is not interested in risking their heart again. But there are also people who prefer to not have this type of relationship and instead are focused on other non-romantic relationships in their life. Still, it's important to note that a character's sexuality is not the important part, but rather how they feel about that state and how they integrate it into their sense of self.

Now for a moment assume your character has a loving relationship in their life. Characters who are in loving relationships will have these as a priority and also as a driver of their behaviour. This is why so many thrillers are based on the idea that the bad guy has kidnapped (or killed) the main character's loved one. There's a backlash against the idea of having female characters who exist for no other reason than to be in peril (or die horribly at the start) in order to motivate the hero to go out and do some butt kicking.

As a writer don't use a loving relationship as a cheat for motivation. Make sure that character has her own purpose. (And, if you ever want me to read your books, please don't put the dog in peril—I can't handle it.)

Your Turn

- Is your character married or in a long-term relationship? How would they describe that relationship?
- What is your character's relationship history? Are there any relationships that they regret?
- Is your character (happy / satisfied / unhappy)with their current relationship status?

SOCIAL SUPPORTS AND FRIENDSHIPS

Examples of questions that fall into this area of a counselling interview:

- Tell me about your friends.
- Do you belong to a church?
- Do you belong to other organizations (writer's groups, running groups, knitting circles)?
- Do you regularly volunteer with any organizations? If yes, which one(s)?
- Do you have someone to turn to if you are facing challenges?

Why this information is important

No man is an island. Research shows poor social support has been linked to depression, cardiovascular disease and altered brain chemistry. And you don't need research to know that social supports help during times of stress. This might be practical supports like bringing over soup when you're sick, lending someone money, or emotional support such as listening to someone who needs to talk during a difficult time. Friends who bring chocolate and are willing to curse out your foes are those who should be treasured. People who show up with a tarp, a shovel and no questions are one in a million.

Some individuals have a wide circle of friends, others a much smaller circle. This is a case where size doesn't necessarily matter, but what does matter, is the quality of these relationships. Anyone who has ever had a real crisis in their life quickly discovers who they can truly count on when things are down. Many people have had an emergency only to discover people they thought would always have their back have faded away when needed.

A large circle of support is another resource for your character. This provides them with people in their life who may be able to do things to assist them in the pursuit of their goal. This might be the best friend who also happens to be a computer hacker or a friend at church who will let them hide out at their house if they're in danger. Again, with any positive support, you as the writer may have to take this away from your character if you need them to tackle a problem on their own. (There's that serial killer tendency popping up again.)

When your character needs emotional support and has to talk things over with a friend, this gives you as the writer a lot of opportunities. You might use this section of dialogue to provide critical information about the plot, show change in the character's emotional functioning, or show how a character views the world.

Your Turn

- How would your character describe their social circle?
- Who is their "go to" person for when they are struggling?
- Is your character someone others rely on for support?

PERCEPTION OF THE HEALTH OF RELATIONSHIPS

Examples of questions that fall into this area of a counselling interview:

- How do you get along with the people in your life?
- For people who you've fallen out with, why do you think that's happened?
- Have the relationships in your life changed over time?
- How would your friends describe you?
- How would a co-worker describe you?
- Who do you go to when there are challenges?

Why this information is important

Questions in this area often provide insight into how well the character understands himself and his interaction with others. Relationships are one way we define ourselves. (I'm a mother. I'm the eldest son. etc.) Family is chosen for us, but there's the saying that friends are the family you choose. So, who do your characters choose to have in their life? And do they choose wisely?

We tend to be slightly different when we're with different people. There's who we are with co-workers, which may be very different from the person our closest friends see. And how many of us have been shocked to see an adult partner suddenly revert to a child when they go home to see family? A counsellor wants to understand all those different facets of a person, so we can put it into one overall reflection of who a person is.

Your Turn

- If your character was asked about their relationship history, what would they say?
- How would your character's best friend describe them? Would this be different between a childhood best friend and someone who knows them in the present day?

RELIGION

Examples of questions that fall into this area of a counselling interview:

- Did you grow up with a particular faith?
- Would you describe yourself as religious?
- If you don't practice any particular organized religion, would you describe yourself as spiritual where you believe there is some outside force or entity that is otherworldly in some way?
- How important are your beliefs to your everyday life?
- How would your religion view the situation you're currently in?

Why this information is important

Religion can be a significant way that individuals make sense of the world and the challenges they face. They may rely on prayer or rituals to assist them with coping. If you believe in the afterlife and a loved one dies, you may take comfort in the idea that they have gone to a "better place" or that you will re-join them later. Conversely, you may be angry at God for taking away someone you cared about. Individuals with strong religious beliefs may have those beliefs drive the actions they take, how they view themselves, and their view of others. Because religion is such a cornerstone issue for many, it's also a potential source of conflict.

As a counsellor, I want to know if an individual has deeply held beliefs since they may impact (either positively or negatively) their progress. This is also true from the writing perspective. A character with a set belief structure may gain peace from it, be tormented by it, or be driven to conflict with another person because of it.

Your Turn

- What is your character's religious background?
- Do they still believe in the faith they were raised in?
- Would others describe your character as spiritual?
- What does your character think happens to people after they die? Do they believe in heaven and hell?

EDUCATION AND HOBBIES

Examples of questions that fall into this area of a counselling interview:

- What is your level of education?
- What do you see as your areas of strength/weakness?
- In what areas would you describe yourself as knowledgeable?
- Would you describe yourself as a "lifelong learner?"
- Have you taken any courses, or learned anything new in the past couple of years?
- Did you enjoy school?
- Do you have any learning disabilities?
- What do you do for joy?
- How do you spend your free time?
- Are you able to drive, or have an active driver's license?

Why this information is important

For counsellors, questions in this area help provide additional details about what skills may be important to an individual's personal growth, or areas that may be more challenging. For example, an individual with a significant learning disability may have more trouble going back to school to train in a new field compared to someone who doesn't have one. Someone who doesn't have a driver's license has a different kind of problem with returning to school depending on the town's access to public transit. It can also hint to a counsellor how open someone is to new things, as well as what might give them some joy.

For a writer, education and hobbies have a practical impact: they provide the character with resources they can use to solve problems and move toward their goal. If your character knows how to fix a car, that might be critically important in a chase scene. There's a reason that Katniss in *The Hunger Games* is shown early in the book to be skilled in archery. Later her ability is going to be a matter of life and death.

Education will also likely have an impact on how your character speaks. Word choice and vocabulary is one way that we can tell characters apart when they're speaking. People who work in specific industries or have specific hobbies often use jargon or slang. This can add to the feel of the novel, making the characters more realistic. For example, a young kid who sees someone have a heart attack may say something like "he keeled right over, like a troll going down." An ER nurse will call it a "myocardial infarction with sudden cardiac arrest." Both of those reactions tell us about the character and add to the scene.

Your Turn

- If their teachers were to fill out a form on your character what would they say? (i.e. Susan talks too much in class.) Do a report card for your character.
- If your character could take a class for fun, what would they take? Why?
- When your character thinks back on school, what memories stick out?

HEALTH

Examples of questions that fall into this area of a counselling interview:

- What is your overall health?
- What is your fitness level?
- What do you do for exercise?
- Do you have any disabilities?
- If you do have a disability, please describe it to me including how it impacts you.
- What's been your experience with the health care industry?
- Do you smoke?
- Are you at a healthy weight?
- Has there been any change in your health?

Why this information is important

There's little doubt that a mind-body connection exists. How we feel physically impacts our mood. Anyone who has had a severe headache and still had to go to work, or can't sleep well due to pain, can tell you that it can be darn hard in those circumstances to remain plucky or focused. However, we know that this interaction also goes the other way. People who are under a lot of stress are more susceptible to colds or the flu. People who are in emotional distress often report higher levels of pain as compared to people who are emotionally in a good place.

As a counsellor, I'm intrigued by how an individual interprets their health and perception of functioning. Are they accurate or do they over- or under-estimate their ability? For example, an individual may downplay their challenges because they don't want to be seen as potentially weak, or not fit with their personal image of what it means to be (insert their role here—father, wife, CEO, etc.).

In contrast, there are individuals who underestimate their abilities. In those cases, I'm wondering what they gain by this decision. For example, have you ever had a cold that seemed so horrid on a Monday morning that you had no choice but to go back to bed and miss work? But the same cold on a day of vacation meant you still went out and had fun? The cold is the same. In theory, your ability to cope with it should be the same, but when it means you might miss a chance to enjoy part of your holiday you find new reserves. To be clear this doesn't mean that the individual is necessarily trying to "game" the system or lie, but that our perception of our abilities can change depending on the situation.

In the field I worked in, this tendency to under-represent your abilities, or to appear more ill than your objective health status, was referred to as "secondary gain." This is commonly discussed in legal circles. Examples included an individual who may have been in a car accident and sustained some significant injuries. While medically they had a good recovery, they might still report higher levels of pain and challenges with certain tasks. If that individual was involved in a lawsuit where there was potential for court-ordered financial compensation, it would be impossible for the individual not to understand at some level that if they had increased difficulties, they may get a larger settlement.

The same individual may have also been the primary person in their relationship who did all the heavy lifting to run the home, cooking, cleaning and childcare. Since they were injured, their partner may have stepped up and taken on more tasks and been more focused on them and caring for them. Giving up that attention can be hard. The person may fear, at either an unconscious or conscious level, that if they got better they may find themselves buried under a lot of work again. *And all that attention has been darn nice!* They gain something by being ill. Again, they may be unaware of the influence on how they feel, but it's important for a counsellor to understand.

As the author of your story, this information about health is also important for story development. A character's health or level of disability may impact their ability to react in different situations. A character who is blind will have challenges that characters who have perfect vision do not. However, someone who is blind and has had to navigate a seeing world has also developed some coping skills and resilience that may be very useful if they're presented with a challenge in a different area. A character's health status may also be important to story development, requiring them to interact with certain people (nurses, doctors)—or their ill health may actually be the start of the zombie apocalypse.

Exercise care and diligence if writing about characters with health issues or disabilities, just as you would when writing about a character who may be a different race or come from a cultural background different from yours. Don't rely on tropes or clichés. People with disabilities are people first. And if you don't have direct experience with a disability, consider hiring a sensitivity reader.

Your Turn

- What would your character's doctor say about them and their health?
- What ownership do they take for their health? Do they take the blame for something they can't control? (i.e. I got cancer because I'm somehow a bad person.)
- Consider how your character reacts to any health

challenges. Do they under- or over-represent their abilities? Are there issues of secondary gain for them? If so, what are they, and is the character aware of it?

WORK AND EMPLOYMENT

Examples of questions that fall into this area of a counselling interview:

- Where did you work as a teen?
- What is your work history?
- What duties did you do in those jobs?
- What is the length of time in those roles?
- Have you ever been promoted?
- Have you ever been fired from a job? Why?
- Have you ever quit a job? Why?
- How do you get along with your co-workers?
- How do you get along with managers and supervisors?
- How do you feel about your current position?
- Do you like your job?

Why this information is important

One of the first questions adults tend to ask one another when meeting is, "What do you do?" The majority of adults spend the bulk of their day at work (paid or unpaid work such as being a full-time parent). This is often a large part of how we define ourselves. "I'm an engineer." "I'm a cashier." And it's not just how we define ourselves, it's also how we make sense of other people. If you hear that someone is a doctor who does heart transplants on infants, you make judgements about them. They must be really smart, they're hardworking, they bring a lot to the community.

Conversely, if you hear someone is a dishwasher you may assume that they weren't smart or hard-working enough to get a more challenging job. We make value judgements about people based on their work. This value judgement can vary. One person hears that someone is a writer and thinks: *Wow, they're so artistic! They create entire worlds, that's amazing!* Someone else hears writer and thinks: *Please, they play with imaginary friends all day? Why don't they get a real job instead of hanging out in PJs all the time?"* Clearly, the person who views writers negatively has never had the joy of working in PJs all day. Pants are overrated.

As a counsellor, I'm also interested in how well people function in workplaces. An individual who shares a work history that is all short-term employment and leaves those jobs because they either quit or are fired over and over (and over) is a red flag for me (and also likely future employers). This type of work history makes me wonder if they have trouble getting along with others, if there are behaviour issues, or if they are unable to commit.

A work history also provides a list of skills and abilities. As a counsellor who specialized in working with people with disabilities, one of my primary roles was looking at what skills and abilities an individual had prior to an accident or illness that they might be able to repurpose if they no longer were capable of doing their original occupation. For example, with a truck driver who has a back injury and can't sit for long periods, I might look into transportation logistics (planning trucking routes) as a new career option.

As a writer, your character's occupation may have story importance and may put them into certain situations. For instance, a doctor's knowledge of medicine may help them stop the zombie spread. A spy will have a different typical day than most people who work as receptionists (although to be fair being a receptionist and having to deal with the public all day, is its own level of harrowing).

You may also play with reader expectations. For example, you may be writing a character who is a funeral director, but rather than serious and solemn, you make your director have a cutting sense of humour. There's a common intersection between personality and occupation. There are individuals who are well-suited to what they do because it matches who they are as people. There are entire books based on this idea, *Do What You Are* by Paul Tieger and Barbara Barron-Tieger helps individuals who are in the process of career exploration by having them look at their Myers-Briggs profile (a personality measure discussed later in this book) and match it to specific occupations.

Your Turn

- Do a resume for your character. With what they have done in the past, were they good at that role?
- What skills do they have?
- Who was your character's favourite boss (or least favourite)? Why?
- How long did they stay in various occupations and what were the reasons (perhaps real and what they admit to) for why they stayed or left?
- What was your characters favourite job? Least favourite? Why?

SUMMARY

A formal counselling interview is a great way to get to know your characters over a broad range of topics. Think about how your characters would respond to the different questions, both what they *would* say and what they *wouldn't* say.

Your Turn

- Choose a few of the questions and interview your character. Or for a different twist, have someone else select questions and interview you where you respond from your character's POV. Record this so you don't have to pause and write down notes. Let the answers be spontaneous. You might be surprised at what you say.

6

HOW CAN A TIMELINE TOOL SIMPLIFY BACKSTORY?

When I was in graduate school one of our professors taught us a tool that was simple and direct. Over my career, I used this tool almost daily and often when meeting clients for the first time. It provided a way to quickly understand where a person was coming from and the meaning of different events in their life.

The tool is a simple timeline. I would draw a line down a sheet of paper. On the top of the line I would write **birth** and on the bottom, I'd write **today**. Then I'd ask individuals to list what major events happened in their life as a way for me to get to know them. If they felt it was a positive event, they'd list it on the left of the line; if it was negative, they'd write it to the right of the line.

For example, here's what a basic timeline from someone's life might look like:

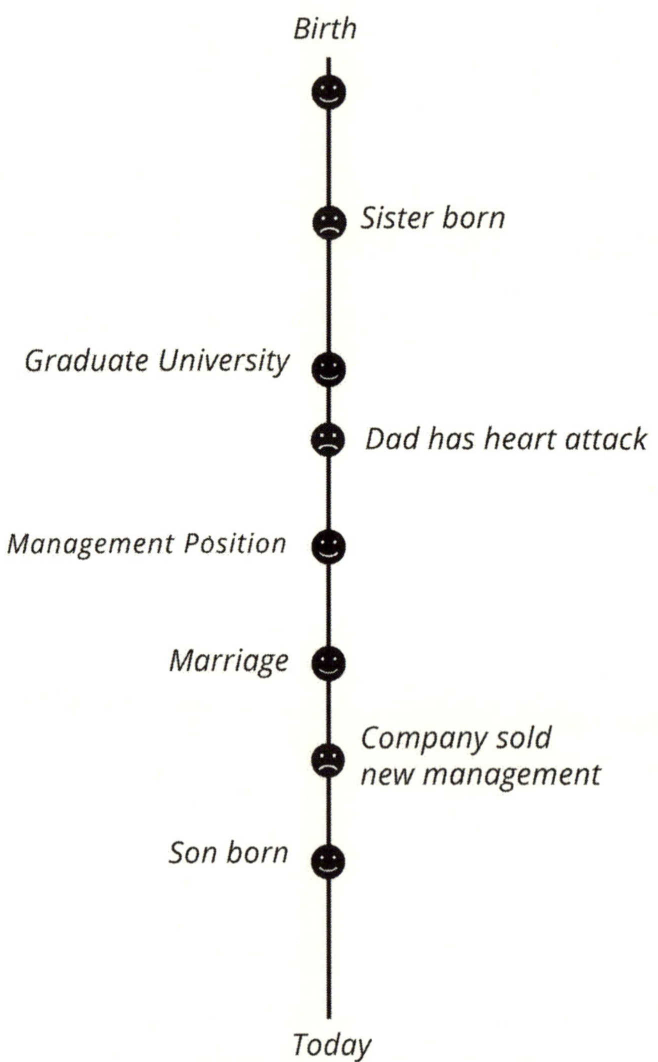

Sample timeline tool from someone's life.

There were multiple purposes for doing this exercise. What was interesting to me wasn't just what they saw as major milestones in their life, although it did provide a short and quick snapshot of those events. More importantly it gave me some insight into how they *perceived* those events.

For example, I've had people list university graduation as a major event, and others (who are also university grads) not list it. Perhaps they never doubted they would go to college so it wasn't seen as a big deal. Another person may list it as a major event, talking about how they were the first in their family to go, or possibly they had a learning disability so completing university felt like a huge accomplishment.

In the example above you'll notice that they listed the birth of their sister as a negative event. When asked, they may talk about how their sister was born with a disability and as a result, took a lot of their parents' time and attention. While they love their sister, it also brought a lot of stress (both financial and emotional) to the family. They're proud of finishing university and getting a career going. They also saw their marriage as a positive event. The change in management at work is a negative for them and that might be the issue that they needed to discuss in counselling. They'd always seen their job as a positive, but now things have changed and it's causing trouble in their home life.

The timeline allows me to see what is important to them and how the issues from their past (worries about financial issues and family strife) might be impacting the choices they make about work in the present.

I once worked with a young man who was a roofer. While at work, he accidentally fell into hot tar. Because tar is sticky, he was unable to quickly remove himself from the source of the burn, as you would when you yank away from a hot stove. Due to pain, he snapped his safety line and then ran off the roof, falling four stories to the ground, where he landed and was impaled on a wrought iron fence.

As a result, he sustained third degree burns, major orthopaedic injuries (crushed vertebra, compound fracture of the femur), also internal injuries including a ruptured spleen. I met this person as he was going through a very painful rehab process. Then to top it off, his girlfriend left him because she couldn't deal with the burn scars. It was clear that this young man would have lifelong physical impacts that would prevent him from doing roofing, or any other manual labour occupations, which was all he had done in the past.

I did this exercise with him and he listed the accident TO THE LEFT OF THE LINE as a positive event in his life. My first thought was—*uh-oh, he's also got a head injury on top of everything else.* So, I asked him about it. He replied: *"I'm only 26, but because of this accident I know who my real friends are and who I can count on. Most people go their entire lives without knowing."*

Think about that. Think about what kind of person has this experience and then describes it in this way. As soon as he spoke, I knew this guy would be okay in the long-term. His view of this event gave me a sense of how he would move forward. This isn't to say that I didn't think he would struggle and have challenges, rather that his attitude was going to assist in carrying him through those difficult times to when he would be on the other side. If he were a character and I put him in a dire circumstance, this backstory would impact how he'd react. I also suspect it would impact how the reader viewed him. He's a remarkable young man and his attitude makes it very difficult not to cheer for him to be successful.

Here are two examples of what a timeline might look like for two very different characters. In both cases these are timelines that happen between birth and the start of the book. They do not include story events.

Katherine (Women's Fiction)

Positive/left of line: Baby sister was born, moved to Boston, got an art scholarship, met Austin, graduated university, got job in law firm, got married, bought dream house, had baby.

Negative/right of line: was in car accident with significant broken bones, had to transfer schools due to being bullied, sister became an addict, baby died from SIDS.

Katherine (Women's Fiction) sample timeline.

Possible impact: If the novel is about Katherine getting divorced from Austin and then moving to Paris to rediscover her love of painting, versus hating being a lawyer, you can see how the backstory may play out. The loss of her sister to addiction and her own child to SIDS may make her reluctant to create close ties with others. She may struggle with feeling life is unfair and feeling somehow responsible for the bad things that happened to her. She did everything right and yet things still went badly so now (in this book) she's going to remember that life has passion and love and colour.

Nymgarten (Adult Science Fiction)

Positive/left of line: Born into off-world family, got first flyer for holiday, accepted into Star Academy, paired with Dougan for flight school and eventual first posting.

Negative/right of line: Parents split up, failed first attempt at Star Academy entrance exam, mentor died, war broke out.

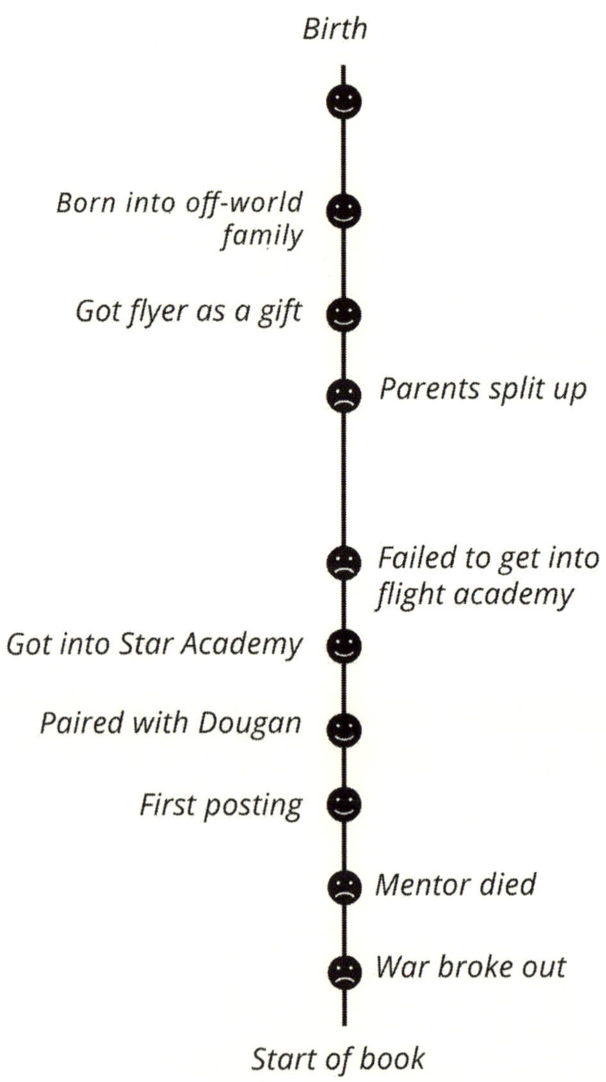

Nymgarten (Adult Science Fiction) example timeline.

Possible impact: This book is the story of cocky fly-boy Nym growing up and taking on a leadership role to take his people to victory in a war that risks them all. He likely comes across as cocky and arrogant, but deep down readers will know because of his backstory that he has a heart of gold. (Yes, I did have a serious Han Solo crush growing up.) Part of what will challenge Nym in this book is getting over his sense of entitlement from his childhood and accepting that the death of his mentor really shocked his sense of how the world works. However, the bonds he made with Dougan and the "out of the box" way he approached flight school (told in flashbacks and dialogue) will leave the reader excited to see how he'll approach this battle and save the day.

Your Turn

- Create a timeline for your character. The dot on the top is their birth. The dot on the bottom is the start of the story. What's happened to them? How do they view each life milestone?
- You can also create a timeline where the dot at the top is the start of your book and the dot at the bottom is the end of your story. Write down the major events that happen to your character in the plot, but also take note of how they view those events. Does the character list them to the right or left on the line?
- If you created a timeline, look through it. What

have you learned about your character? What major events did they think to list? Are there any that they didn't list, but you as the author see as very important to who they are?

- You can also explore these events more fully. One way to do this is to write a journal entry from the character's POV (even if you're not using the first person to tell the story) the day or day after that event.
- Write a journal entry from the POV of another character who might share a memory of an event with your character. How do they see it? The same? Differently? What new perspective do they bring?
- Create timelines for your antagonist or other major characters in the story. How has what's happened to them impacted the choices and decisions they make in your story?

7

WHAT DO YOU DO WITH ALL THAT BACKSTORY?

We've spent a lot of time exploring character backstory and the impact that has on who they are at the start of the book and the reactions and decisions they make during the story. You now have a richer understanding of what key things happened to your character in their past and likely more empathy for who they are and some of their choices.

So, what are you going to do with all of this great information?

What I'm about to say may discourage you, but all this work you've done to think of backstory, to come up with all the sensory details… yeah, you likely won't use all of it in your manuscript. Wait! Don't throw this book against the wall! That process was still beneficial. Much of this material will just be there to help *you*. When you're writing and a character faces a choice you will have a better idea why they may do A versus B. The reader likely won't need to know all the ins and outs, but you do.

Some details of backstory aren't necessarily important for the plot. For example, J.K. Rowling revealed long after the original *Harry Potter* books were out, that Dumbledore was gay. This caused controversy with some people feeling that she was in some way "messing" with characters after the fact, possibly in an effort to be more politically correct. Others felt that this was a critical detail that should have been mentioned in the story because it made them like the character more. However, since Dumbledore's sexuality wasn't relevant to the original story, it wasn't included. But J.K. Rowling is clear, knowing Dumbledore's sexuality shaped who he was and the choices he made.

It's okay for you to know things the reader doesn't. Because you are the architect of your story you need to know all the things—the soil composition to make sure the foundation is solid, what's behind every wall, the electrical map, and what kind of grout was used on the tile in the bathroom. Although the reader is going to live in your house they don't need that level of detail, but they need to have faith that electricity will flow from the socket. You may at times peel away a portion of the wall to let them see how things work, but you won't do it all the time. Never fear, the time and energy you spent on developing your characters' backstories won't be wasted.

8

THE DREADED INFO DUMP

Because we love backstory and all the interesting details we came up with, there is a tendency to want to share all of it with the reader. This is known as "the dreaded info dump." There is a particular risk of falling prey in the opening chapters where we desperately want the reader to know ALL THE THINGS. We fear if the reader doesn't know everything we know, the story won't make sense to them. The problem is that the reader doesn't need to know this level of information, or at least not at the start. And including too much backstory runs the risk of slowing the pace of your story.

It's useful to remember that any time you go back to the past to share backstory you are essentially stopping the forward flow of the story. Imagine your readers are in a car, your main character at the wheel, zooming along a highway in the pursuit of their story goal. When you pause to give backstory details your main character stops the car, pops it in reverse, backing up to show the readers something, and then puts the car back into drive and continues the trip. There are times when stopping the car to share a bit of information makes the entire trip make more sense, and there are other times when the people in the car will become annoyed because they were promised a trip to a specific destination, and your character doesn't seem to be going there. If your dad was the kind to pull over on a family road trip and make you look at some random historical marker or see the world's biggest ball of twine, you know how annoying it can be when you just want to get to the hotel with the pool. (And yes dad, I know you stopped so that I could learn things.)

9

HOW DO YOU DECIDE WHAT IS IMPORTANT?

When you're uncertain what backstory to include in the story, consider:

- How does what happened in the past link to what is happening in the main storyline?
- Are there details that the reader *must* know in order to understand the plot?
- Is your character's reaction to something in the past so unusual that the reader may not understand it unless you show it on the page?
- Other than backstory, how does your character's motivation come through?
- With the backstory, what is the minimum the reader needs to know?
- If you cut the backstory from the manuscript would the reader notice it?

If you still aren't sure what to include consider doing "A/B testing." That is, have four to six beta readers go through your manuscript. Give half of them a version with the more extensive backstory and the other half the version without. Ask them their perceptions of the character's motivations (Did you understand why character X did Y?) and pacing (Were there places where you considered putting the book down, where you lost interest in the story?). Comparing the two different feedback streams may tell you which version of the story works better.

10

WEAVING IN BACKSTORY

Now that you know what kind of backstory you want to include you have some different options about how to integrate it. We'll discuss three of the most common ways to weave it in.

Dialogue

One of the easiest ways to include backstory is to have characters share intimate or revealing details of their pasts with each other. For example, Joe turns to his best friend Lars as they stand at a window. They're being chased by bad guys. The only way to escape is to go out the window, shimmy along the ledge and go into the window of the office next door. Lars is already starting to open the window. Joe tells him, "I suppose now isn't the best time to tell you that I've always been terrified of heights. Long story, but I can't do it. I'll hold them off here, you go on."

Lars may or may not leave Joe behind to shoot it out with the bad guys, but it's important that the reader know that even though it makes way more sense for Joe to go out the window, he's going to choose to stay inside and hope for the best in the gun battle. Assuming Joe survives you can bet the reader is going to want to know what happened to Joe that made him more willing to face bullets than a ledge.

One of the ways that we deepen relationships with friends or romantic interests is by being vulnerable and disclosing information about ourselves. You might create a scene where two characters are getting to know each other and swapping stories about their past (either funny or painful or both.) At the time, the reader may not know the importance of that story, but later when a character takes a specific action or makes a choice the reader will reflect back and see where the source of motivation may have come from.

If you choose to have backstory revealed in dialogue, ensure that you avoid the "as you know" syndrome. This is when two characters discuss something that both of them already know, not because they have any interest in talking about it, but because the author needs the reader to have that information. For example,

> "As you know Brian, we were twins separated at birth who didn't meet again until two years ago," Clarence said, stroking his moustache.

The reason this line doesn't work is because Brian would know that he and Clarence were brothers. He'd wonder why in the world Clarence was telling him this now. Even if the reader doesn't recognize it as an info dump, it will feel "off" to them. Also stroking a moustache is slightly creepy.

Another variation of the "as you know" is the "as you don't know." In this situation a character tells another character key information that the other character doesn't know, but where it makes no logical sense for them to share that information.

The classic example of this is when the bad guy has the good guy tied up and declares, "I'm about to kill you, but before I do let me tell you all about my nefarious plan to destroy the world and why I've done this horrible thing." Then the bad guy lays out all the key information that will be needed moments later when the good guy manages to get away and has to stop the plan from happening. Again, even though the reader may not know what this is called, it reads as inauthentic to them. They can sense that they're being manipulated and they're not going to like it.

In general, when we talk about dialogue as a way to show backstory, we're thinking about two (or more) characters talking to each other. However, depending on your story, you may have a character engaging in internal dialogue. They may remind themselves of something that happened in the past or even have an internal argument about it. Internal dialogue often leads to one of the most common ways to share backstory—the flashback.

The flashback

A flashback is when an experience or encounter triggers a vivid recollection. You've likely had this experience in your own life. Something happens, and you are instantly reminded of something in your past. Flashbacks can be positive or negative.

For example, you stroll around a corner and there's a bakery. The smell of the hot bread transports you back to when you were a child, staying at your grandmother's home where she made fresh bread in the mornings. In that instant of remembering, you might hear her voice, remember how her eyes crinkled up when she smiled and that she always wore that giant fuzzy navy-blue robe first thing in the morning. You may recall the oil painting she had on the wall that she said was her grandparents' farm in Ireland. Emotions may come back for you—making you feel safe, warm, loved, and protected. At your grandmother's you felt genuinely cared for.

The negative version would be something like a person grabs your elbow when you almost trip at work. Instantly you recall how your dad would go into rages when he'd been drinking and if you dared to try to walk away, he'd grab your elbow and yank you back. You might recall the sour-sweet smell of beer on his breath. How his face was covered in whiskers and his eyes bloodshot. The sound of the smack of flesh when he hit you still rings in your ears. You may even have an instant response where you lurch backwards or flail out against a co-worker who was just trying to help.

Because flashbacks often have strong emotional connotations, they allow you as the writer to share those emotions and motivations with the reader in context.

A flashback in fiction is when the regular forward narrative is put on pause and the character or author goes back in time. To ensure that the reader knows what is happening and isn't confused, you need to signal that a flashback is happening. This can be done by a space break, transitional line or change in font. At times you'll see all three happening. For example,

Linda pulled on the coat. It smelled musty, as if it had been locked up in an attic for years. It made her think back to when she was a child. (this is a transitional line)

(extra space break before the flashback scene) and (font change)

"Why can't I get a coat at the mall?" Linda asked, stamping her foot on the tile floor.

"Because we can't afford new things," her mom replied with a tired sigh. "Besides they have lots of nice coats here."

Linda looked around the thrift store. Clothing was shoved so tightly on the racks that you could hardly see what was there. It smelled of old people, discarded crusty Kleenex and mold. It didn't matter what her mom said. There were no nice coats here —just things no one wanted anymore. Like her and her mom.

(extra space break after the flashback scene) then (transitional line)

Linda shook her head to clear the image away. She wasn't in a thrift store anymore and if she didn't want to borrow a coat, she didn't have to. One the benefits of being wealthy meant not having to do things you didn't want to do.

Parallel time frames

The third most common way to integrate backstory into a manuscript is through parallel time frames. This is a story structure choice, where you will have a character's story unfold in an early time contrasted with a current time. For example, you have rotating chapters between a character as a child during the war and the same character as an old man in the present day. Perhaps there is a mystery about something that happened at the end of the war that is unravelling in the present time and the author goes back and forth between the two timelines.

This kind of structure has been used by the authors Kate Morton (*The House at Riverton*), Christina Baker Kline (*The Orphan Train*), and Kristin Hannah (*The Nightingale*.) This allows you to tell a very particular type of story. In these stories, backstory is doing much more than just fleshing out a character. What has happened in the past is critically important to the main, present-day storyline. If you were to cut out the past portion of the story, the entire book would fail. As a result, you would only use this type of structure in particular circumstances depending on the need of your story.

11

HOW DO BACKSTORY AND PERSONALITY WORK TOGETHER?

This book is based on the premise that knowing backstory is what allows you to create more realistic and three-dimensional characters. Once you know the characters' backstory, you can explore how those events, and more importantly, how your characters interpret those events, impacted their personality.

Deciding on what kind of personality your character has can be a difficult concept to wrap your head around. What do we even mean by the term 'personality?' The American Psychological Association states that personality:

> *"Refers to individual differences in characteristic patterns of thinking, feeling and behaving. The study of personality focuses on two broad areas: One is understanding individual differences in particular personality characteristics, such as sociability or irritability. The other is understanding how the various parts of a person come together as a whole."*

Basically, personality is how you act and interact with the world.

Many psychological theories refer to the 'Big Five' personality traits. This concept is that personalities can be described by variations across five basic dimensions:

1. openness to new experience,
2. conscientiousness,
3. extroversion/introversion,
4. agreeableness and
5. neuroticism.

While this may give you some ideas to consider, you can dig deeper by going into more detail. We'll do that by looking at the concepts of Emotional Intelligence and the Myers-Briggs Type Indicator. These two theories will provide a wider scope to explore the differences between people and how personality might manifest itself.

PART III

EMOTIONAL INTELLIGENCE

12

EMOTIONAL INTELLIGENCE

What is emotional intelligence?

The study of emotional intelligence came about from a basic question: Why do smart people do stupid things? A question you might have asked about people in your own life. It sets up the idea that there may be different kinds of intelligence. That is, that people might be smart in different ways. First, it's helpful to understand what we're discussing, and how IQ (Intelligence Quotient) is different than EQ (Emotional Quotient or another way of saying Emotional Intelligence.)

> Intelligence Quotient (IQ): A measure of an individual's intellectual, analytical, logical and rational abilities. It is concerned with verbal, spatial, visual and mathematical skills. IQ is typically determined by the Wechsler Adult Intelligence Scale (WAIS.)

Given that we have well-researched ways to measure intelligence, logic tells us people who score well on IQ tests should be the most successful, right? That idea may have made you laugh. Most of us are well aware of people who are quite smart, and in theory capable, who make horrible life decisions and choices. These might be people in our own family or a well-known co-worker. (Yes, Doug in accounting, I'm talking about you.) The truth is that common sense doesn't seem so common. If IQ isn't a predictor of success, then researchers knew there must be something else that makes the difference in how people move through life. That led to the concept of emotional intelligence.

> Emotional Quotient (EQ): The non-cognitive abilities, competencies and skills that influence an individual's ability to cope. It includes the ability to perceive, understand and generate emotion. It started with researchers, Salovey, Mayer, and Bar-On. Daniel Goleman is perhaps best known in the world of Emotional Intelligence as he made the concept more popular with his book, *Emotional Intelligence: Why It Can Matter More Than IQ.*

At the most basic level EQ means understanding and having an awareness of your own emotions and how they impact your choices as well as how that might impact others in your life. However, not only does it mean having an awareness of these emotions, but also an ability to *control* those emotions (that can be the tricky part) even when stressed and interacting with others who may also be having strong emotions.

13

HOW EMOTIONAL INTELLIGENCE IS HELPFUL WITH CHARACTER CREATION

Just as the IQ of your character would make a difference in how they tackle problems, speak and interact with others, their EQ also influences how they will act and react. Individuals have a balance of strengths and weaknesses that at times help them and in other situations work against their goals. When you know and understand these strengths and weaknesses, you can use them to either get your character into more trouble or to get them out. You'll be able to create realistic dynamics between them and other characters.

If you're interested in EQ, there is a wealth of information to review. There is a formal test that must be given by a Master's level counsellor or therapist, the EQi, which measures an individual's self-reported functioning on the fifteen different types of Emotional Intelligence. However, there are several less official online versions, many of which are free so you can test yourself. You could also answer the questions as if you were your character to gain additional insight.

There are also a number of books on this topic that deal with specific areas including: *Primal Leadership* (EQ in workplace environments), *Grow Up: A Man's Guide* (EQ and masculinity), and *Six Steps Toward an Emotionally Intelligent Teenager* (EQ to help you survive having teens in the house). These books often include case studies which may assist you in developing your own characters and provide you with tips or suggestions on how someone may improve in select areas.

While EQ is still being researched, there does appear to be a correlation between EQ and success. People who have strong EQ tend to do better in school, at work and in interpersonal relationships. This means as a writer you can use the different aspects of EQ to give your characters both strengths and weaknesses as they navigate toward their goal.

The bad news is that IQ is a static measure, that is, you're not getting any smarter and neither are your characters. You may (and hopefully are) becoming more knowledgeable and educated as you learn new things. However, you will hit a threshold of capability.

For example, my math skills are not the greatest. My high school algebra teacher is now laughing aloud at this understatement. I've taken up to Masters level math courses, but they were always a struggle. (This is also a massive understatement.) I worked harder than other people in my class and still got lower grades. If my goal had been to get a PhD in mathematics, I likely would not have made it. It wasn't a case of effort or having the right teacher—there is simply a limit to my ability and only so far that I could stretch. When writing characters keep in mind what is hard-wired into their intelligence and the areas where they could grow, keeping in mind that within their capacity there is still wriggle room about what they can learn.

IQ tends to decline slightly as we age. This is why IQ tests use age norms. You're compared to others in your own age bracket so that your score stays consistent. Older people are given a bit of a boost in their score compared to people who are younger. Now if that's not depressing for those of us with a birthday coming up, I'm not sure what is.

The good news is that EQ is a flexible trait—you can, and likely do, get better with age. It doesn't come as a surprise to anyone who is a parent that EQ is still developing for children and teens. Your character's EQ, and how it changes over the course of the story, may be one of the ways that you demonstrate their growth and development.

When creating a character for your story one way to begin is by considering the different aspects of emotional intelligence and determining how your character does in those areas. Let's dive in and learn more about this concept.

14

THE 15 MEASURES OF EMOTIONAL INTELLIGENCE

Now let's discuss the fifteen measures of emotional intelligence and look at prompts that might jump start some thoughts on your own character creation. What are the fifteen areas?

1. Emotional Self-Awareness
2. Assertiveness
3. Self-Regard
4. Self-Actualization
5. Independence
6. Empathy
7. Interpersonal Relationships
8. Social Responsibility
9. Problem Solving
10. Reality Testing
11. Flexibility
12. Stress Tolerance
13. Impulse Control

14. Happiness
15. Optimism

These areas are designed to get you thinking. Depending on your character and the situations you put them in during your book some of these may be more useful than others. The goal isn't for you to include all of these aspects in your character, but to help you identify key areas of strength and weakness that will help you shape your characters and their arcs in the story.

After each area there is a list of prompts to get you thinking. I encourage you to do these for your main character, but you may enjoy doing them for all your characters. If a prompt doesn't feel like a good fit, or doesn't intrigue you, skip it and go on to the next.

If you would like an easy way to answer these questions for your characters, you can download the **Character EQ Interview** from our **https://creativeacademyforwriters.com/resources/buildbettercharacters/**page.

EMOTIONAL SELF-AWARENESS

Emotional Self-Awareness: **The ability to recognize your feelings and emotions. Also, the ability to tell the difference between emotions, to know what you're feeling and what caused the feeling.**

We've already discussed that people do not always have awareness about their emotions. It may seem that people *must* know what they feel, but emotions can be confused for one another. For example, an individual who is at the hospital waiting for their child to come out of surgery may lash out at someone who changes the channel on the TV in the waiting room. They may describe themselves as angry, when in reality they're feeling afraid. Or someone may be extremely angry but find themselves crying.

Emotions can have value judgements attached to them. Some emotions can be perceived as negative and this might be why an individual identifies having one emotion over another. This is especially true if an emotion runs counter to how an individual sees themselves. For example, a man who sees himself as strong and very masculine may want to deny feeling fear because if he admitted he was afraid it could throw into question his sense of manhood. In a similar way, a woman who prides herself on being the best mother may not want to admit that she is frustrated and annoyed with her children, because she views that emotion as counter to what it means to be a good mother. (And all of us might think it's time we got past thinking of our gender in such stereotypical ways.)

Your Turn

- On a scale of one to ten, where one is no awareness of their own emotions, and ten is highly aware of emotions, where does your character fall?
- Are there emotions that your character typically confuses with another emotion?
- If there are emotions that your character confuses, what is it about the emotion that they deny that triggers them? Do they have a value judgement about that emotion?
- Is there a story they tell themself that makes them unable to honestly acknowledge what they are feeling?
- When your character feels a strong emotion can they identify what caused it?

ASSERTIVENESS

Assertiveness: **The ability to express your feelings, beliefs and thoughts and stand up for your rights in a non-destructive manner.**

We have all known someone who wouldn't say anything mean no matter what was said or done to them, and others who will fly into a rage at the drop of a hat. Assertiveness is *not* aggression, but rather the ability to express your beliefs or feelings and the willingness to stand up for yourself.

Some individuals feel strongly about various causes or have clear boundaries about what they will accept from others. Other individuals will accept almost any behaviour toward themselves, but if someone were to go after someone they love or a cause that is dear to them, that's what will make them take a stand. For example, a woman may take abuse from others, but when someone is cruel to her child, the mama-bear comes out.

Your Turn

- On a scale of one to ten, where one means your character won't stand up for anything, and ten means that they are fully capable of standing up for themselves, where does your character fall?
- If your character doesn't stand up for themself, why? What do they tell themself when those things happen?
- Are there things that bother your character, that they won't stand up for?
- What are the things that make your character stand up? Is there a line that can't be crossed?

SELF-REGARD

Self-Regard: **The ability to respect and accept yourself as basically good. Recognizing both your positive and negative traits. It can be seen as having self-confidence and a sense of security in who you are.**

No one is all good, or all bad. We're a mix of behaviours. This aspect of emotional intelligence is the concept that you know both your good and bad sides and that overall you see yourself as pretty darn okay. This is not being cocky or arrogant, but rather that you like yourself and have confidence that others should also view you this way. This is an area many people struggle with, on both sides. Either falling into self-doubt and loathing, or conversely thinking they are all that and a box of chocolates.

One of my favourite examples comes from a friend. She was sharing how she'd met someone. He was attempting to woo her and said, "I bet you don't even know how beautiful you are." She turned to him and said, "Oh, I think I do." This example made me laugh out loud and be impressed with her healthy self-regard. She doesn't need a man (or anyone else) to tell her she's beautiful; she knows it.

Your Turn

- On a scale of one to ten, where one means that your character has a horrible self-image (either completely negative or blindly positive) and ten means that they have a positive balanced self-image, where does your character fall?
- What does your character see as their strengths and weaknesses?
- What would other characters say about them? Have the other characters list ten words to describe your main character.
- How many of the descriptions are similar? Do different people in their life see your main character differently?
- Does your main character like themself? Why or why not?
- If your character doesn't like themself, do they talk negatively about themself or do they go the other way making up for insecurity by bragging?

SELF-ACTUALIZATION

Self-Actualization: **The ability to realize one's potential capacities. This is demonstrated by being involved in activities that lead to a full and meaningful life.**

If you took any psychology classes, or read the first section of this book, then you likely remember learning about Maslow's Hierarchy of Needs. This is the theory that people must have their basic needs met, physiological and safety, before they move on to higher aspirations such as esteem and, at the very top, self-actualization. Alas, most people still spend the bulk of their life dealing with day-to-day challenges and have little energy or time left over to seek self-actualization. Heck, some of us are happy if we managed to have something more nutritious than popcorn for dinner. However, someone who scores high in this area has not only identified what gives their life meaning, but is actively going after it.

There are many book and film examples that show this in action, showing a character figuring out what life really means. An example is the Jack Nicholson character in *As Good As It Gets*. (He should also be nicer to dogs in that movie, but I may be biased.)

Your Turn

- On a scale of one to ten, where one means that your character does not pursue anything beyond safety, and ten means that they have pursuits and interests that give meaning to their life, where does your character fall?
- What gives your character's life meaning?
- What is their passion?
- Are they following it? Why or why not?
- Do they believe people approve of their passion?
- Are their basic needs (survival, safety, healthy relationships) being met?
- If your book starts with the character having those basic needs met, and you are taking those away or putting them at risk due to events in your story, how does your character cope?

INDEPENDENCE

Independence: **The ability to be self-directed in your thought process and actions. It's the idea of being free of emotional dependency. Individuals with high scores in this area are able to rely on themselves to plan and make important decisions.**

Does anyone else have a friend who can never decide what restaurant to go to or what to order? *I don't know, where do you want to go? I'm not sure, what are you going to have?* It could be that they honestly don't care what they eat, but it is also possible that they worry that they will make the "wrong" choice. They feel more secure counting on someone else's opinion. Or perhaps you know a person whose identity relies on the approval of others. If their latest social media post doesn't garner sufficient 'likes' it ruins their whole day.

Independence isn't about being a lone wolf, and always going your own way, rather it's about having confidence that you can make your own choices. You know where you want to go in life, and you feel secure in your ability to chart a course to that destination. Your opinion of yourself and your accomplishments (or what you had for dinner and posted on Instagram) doesn't rely on others for approval.

People with high-EQ in this area have the ability to slow down and visualize possible outcomes for their choices versus having a knee-jerk reaction. They recognize that their first thought may not be the best plan, and in fact may result in getting the opposite of what they want. They will weigh the pros and cons of different options and then choose the best.

Your Turn

- On a scale of one to ten, where one means that your character feels incapable of making choices unless others provide a solution or approve of their decisions, and ten means that they're fully capable of making their own choices and seeks input only when and where they feel it will enhance their ability to make a good decision, where does your main character fall?
- Does your character trust their own decisions or do they look to others?

- If they look to others, whose opinion do they seek? Trusted friends or strangers?
- If they trust others to make decisions in their life, have they chosen wisely or do those people have other motivations which may not be in your character's best interest?
- Is your main character capable of pausing before making a choice?

EMPATHY

Empathy: **The ability to be aware of, to understand, and to appreciate the feelings of others. This refers to the ability to "read" others and to show appropriate concern as needed.**

It's not enough to understand your own feelings. People with high EQ scores in this area also understand that others have their own struggles and emotions and can pick up on signals even without being told. For example, a husband comes home and his wife is in the kitchen slamming kitchen cupboards and banging pots and pans on the stove. He asks, "Are you okay?" She glares at him, her left eyelid twitching. "I'm fine," she spits from clenched teeth. "Oh, okay," he responds and then walks out the room to turn on the game. Later he will be perplexed about why she's mad at him. He *asked* her if she was okay. Why didn't she say something if she was upset?

You may know a person who can sense when you're having a bad day and will open up a conversation or do something for you without being asked. These are people we want as friends. They move through the world with an understanding and appreciation of others. They notice others' emotions without being told.

People with strong empathy understand at some level that this skill, in addition to making them appear to be a kind person, can also lead them to what they want. For example, a flight is delayed, and a long line of passengers are dealing with one harried, overworked airline worker. Person after person yells at the customer service clerk, letting him know how upset they are to have their travel plans ruined.

A person with high EQ score in this area will approach the clerk and comment about how they know it's not the clerk's fault and will emphasize how stressful it is. If the clerk has any option over who gets the upgrade on the next flight, who do you think is going to get it? The person who yelled at him, or the person who seemed to understand the situation?

Your Turn

- On a scale of one to ten, where one means that your character hasn't a clue what is happening inside others, and ten means that they are able to read and interpret others' emotions based on non-verbal cues, where does your character fall?
- Is your character "tuned in" to others?
- If they misread the situation, what do they assume?
- If your character is good at reading other's emotions, do they use this power for good, or do they manipulate it to get what they want?
- How does your character feel and respond when they realize that they completely missed how someone was feeling?
- How can your character's failure to recognize someone's subtext and non-verbal cues add conflict to your story?

INTERPERSONAL RELATIONSHIPS

Interpersonal Relationships: **The ability to establish and maintain mutually satisfying relationships that are based on genuine affection and an ability to be your true self with that other person.**

There's significant research that supports the idea that individuals who have healthy relationships (including friends, family and community) describe themselves as happier with their life overall. And if you've ever found yourself in a difficult situation, you know that you'll quickly discover who you can count on and who you can't. It's also satisfying to be the person who can step in and help others when needed. Someone who scores well in this area knows that relationships are a two-way street, that they require work at times, and that it is okay to rely on others when you are the one in need of support.

In a manuscript, knowing who your character has in their life will impact what resources they have available to them. If they only have healthy relationships, your inner Hannibal Lecter may need to come out to remove people from your character's life to leave them on their own in a time of crisis.

Think of books and movies where the mentor character (who's typically better suited to solve any problem) is taken out or for some reason is unable to help. Conversely, if they don't have healthy relationships, the people in their life may be trying to sabotage their efforts to reach their goals. Or the character may be a lone wolf who discovers that having another person at their back comes in handy at times.

The entire romance genre is built on the idea of establishing healthy relationships. If you want to see some anger, give a romance reader a book that you claim is romance, but doesn't deliver a happily ever after. They are reading to see the development of this type of relationship and to see it successfully integrated into a character's life.

Your Turn

- On a scale of one to ten, where one means that your character doesn't have any positive relationships (either that they're alone or that the relationships they do have are toxic), and ten means that they have a strong social support network of friends and family and works to ensure that these relationships remain healthy, where does your character fall?
- What relationships does your character have (family, friends, love)? Are these healthy relationships?
- If you were your character's best friend, what would you think of their relationships?
- How does your character interact with others when they are under stress? Do they lash out, or damage those relationships?
- Does your character believe they deserve good people in their life, or do they sabotage relationships because at some level they don't feel they are worthy?
- When your story heats up and the conflict is raised, what skills do other people in your character's life have that may help them?

- If there is someone in your character's life who is better suited to solve the problem, how can you remove that individual, so your protagonist must solve it themself? (This is why in so many YA (young adult) novels we kill off the parents. If the parents were healthy and helpful the main character would go to them.)
- Create a family tree for your character or a map of other social connections and friends.

SOCIAL RESPONSIBILITY

Social Responsibility: **The ability to be a cooperative, contributing, and constructive member of one's social group. That is a fancy way of saying, you play well with others! This is the ability to act responsibly, even though you may not benefit personally.**

Most of us are part of a larger community. Examples of these communities include religious, writing, knitting, social justice causes, fitness, etc. Being an active member of that community means that at times you must step up—bring something to the potluck, volunteer to lead a session, donate money to a cause, or set-up before or clean-up after an event.

In some manuscripts the call to a higher cause is the main driver of the plot. This is the character who risks all to fight in the resistance, like the middle grade character who stands up to a bully who is tormenting someone else even though they aren't the target. In other manuscripts when the character is finally able to take on another cause, it's a clue to the reader that the character has grown and changed. It's not about the cause itself, it's a demonstration of growth.

An example of this is *The Hunger Games*. In the start of the book/series Katniss' prime goal is survival. As the book progresses she moves from concerns about herself to concerns about the society and she makes herself a revolutionary. There's no doubt at the end of book one that if it was merely about self-survival she would have killed Peeta and won the darn thing by herself. Her willingness to sacrifice is the ultimate example of social responsibility.

Your Turn

- On a scale of one to ten, where one means that your character has no connections to their community that they would sacrifice for (or that they sacrifice far more than they should), and ten means that they have specific community connections where they are an active participating member (even though it may not always result in a direct benefit to them), where does your character fall?
- What causes are important to your character?
- Who, or for what will your character sacrifice their wishes and needs?

- What is your character risking by taking on this cause? Is there a way to increase those stakes?
- Does your character volunteer time or money to any causes?
- How far would your character go to help a group larger than themself?
- How do the people around your character feel about their sacrifices? Do they support the character or resent them?

PROBLEM SOLVING

Problem Solving: **The ability to identify and define problems as well as to come up with and put in place potentially effective solutions.**

Coping with problems is a multiple step process and step one is trickier than you might imagine. First, you have to recognize that there is, in fact, a problem you have to do something about. While some people may labour under the idea that everything is fine even from the middle of a dumpster fire, others will be aware that things aren't going well, but won't see there are steps that they could take to address the issue.

The second step in the problem solving process is generating solutions, not merely reacting, but actually weighing possible options. The final step is putting an option into action, and then measuring the outcome to determine if you need to try again.

In manuscripts, characters are often presented with a problem as an inciting event. If you're familiar with the concept of the Hero's Journey, then you know that many people, when presented with a problem, will refuse that call. In most manuscripts, your character will try different solutions and fail before they successfully beat or solve the challenge in front of them.

Readers are drawn to problems in books. It's human nature to wonder what we would do in those instances and to either be impressed with the character's choices or shake our heads at their stupidity. We want to see characters boxed in and be left to wonder how they will ever get themselves out.

Your Turn

- On a scale of one to ten, where one means that your character has horrid problem-solving abilities, and ten means that they are able to identify and respond to problems, where does your character fall?
- How does your character cope with problems? Would others describe them as a problem-solver?
- Do they even know that they have a problem? Or do they think things are out of their control?
- Are you sure the problem is something they can do something about? You want your character to have agency (the capacity to act).
- Unless you're writing a short story, your character

likely won't solve the problem on the first try, or if they do solve that problem it creates a whole host of new problems. What happens if their first solution doesn't work? What new problems might come out of their actions?

- What is the impact of the attempted solutions on others in the story? You can increase conflict if your character's solution to a problem puts someone or something else they cherish, at risk.

REALITY TESTING

Reality Testing: **The ability to understand the connection between what is experienced and what objectively happened. This means understanding that you see the world through a unique filter, one built from your experiences, values and perspective. And equally important, understanding that others may not view it the same way.**

People with higher EQ scores in this area pause before responding to explore how their views might be impacting how they are seeing a situation. People with lower EQ in this area tend to make false assumptions in the heat of emotion. For example, they may assume there is a negative intent behind what someone else has done. At the extreme far side of the scale would be individuals with mental health challenges impacting their ability to discern the difference between reality and possible hallucinations (auditory or visual).

Reality testing is the basis of every romantic comedy you've ever seen. The character has decided that it is time to declare their feelings to the love interest. They swoop downstairs, giddy and excited, and then (*gasp!*) see the love interest hugging another person (cue tears.) The character realizes that the love interest was only playing with them so they give that love interest the cold shoulder. Chaos and misunderstandings ensue to general hilarity. Then for the big reveal at the end of the movie, it comes out that the love interest was merely comforting a cousin (or another innocuous person) and that in fact, they do love your main character (cue happy music and credits).

Reality testing also works well in any kind of mystery or thriller where the character observes or learns something and assigns a meaning to it, which later is discovered to have a different or opposite meaning. This allows the author to create red herrings that lead the reader astray, so they don't solve the mystery too early in the story.

In virtually every genre there are plot reasons why a writer may want either the character or the reader to be misled by what is seen or interpreted in the story, versus what has objectively happened.

Your Turn

- On a scale of one to ten, where one means that your character is unable to differentiate between reality and their personal experiences, and ten means that they understand the impact of their own filter on their perceptions of the world around them, where does your character fall?
- What does your character believe about the things that happen to them?
- Are their beliefs accurate?
- Is it their interpretation alone of what happened, or are others trying to manipulate the situation to have your character believe something that isn't true?
- How do they act based on their beliefs?
- If the same situation were to be seen by or happen to another character, what would that other character believe about the situation?
- Does your character have good insight into how their own filter impacts how they see the world, or do they think they're completely objective?

FLEXIBILITY

Flexibility: **The ability to adjust your feelings, thoughts, and behaviour to changing situations and conditions. To go with the flow as needed.**

I have a friend who won't do things on a Monday night because Monday night is library night. That's the evening that she returns her books and picks out a new stack for the week ahead. I've tried pointing out that she could go another night, or heck even on her lunch break, but she remains firm—Monday is for the library. Far be it for me to get between someone and their access to books.

While my friend may be a bit more rigid than many, the truth is that people tend to like routines and for her a library routine on Monday nights works. When you check into a hotel do you instantly claim "your side" of the bed? Or perhaps you go into the public washroom in your office and feel a flare of annoyance that someone is in "your stall" even though there are other open stalls?

Humans like to build routines as it allows us to give our lives structure. And most of the time this structure can work for us. However, there are times when we have to be flexible, to change our responses to a new situation because our previous reactions are no longer effective. In most manuscripts, you'll be throwing your character into a wide range of new situations, even if you're not doing a road trip book or a fish out of water theme. Your character will have to respond to these new situations and potentially to new people in their life. Their ability to be flexible will have an impact on their success.

Will your character be someone who recognizes that what they used to do isn't working any longer? Or will they rigidly hold on to old patterns, beliefs or actions? Flexibility is fundamentally the ability to adapt.

Your Turn

- On a scale of one to ten, where one means that your character can't flex at all no matter the situation, and ten means that they are able to flex their responses depending on their environment or the people around them, where does your character fall?
- How does your character deal with the unexpected or unfamiliar?

- How do they feel about change?
- If your character's approach to challenges no longer works, are they able to shift and try new solutions?
- Write a description of your character's ordinary world, what their life and routines look like before your story starts.

STRESS TOLERANCE

Stress Tolerance: **Ability to withstand challenging events and stressful situations without falling apart by using healthy coping strategies.**

In my previous day job, we made our admin assistant our emergency coordinator in charge of preparation for a wide range of possible situations. She was terrific at making sure our First Aid kit was up-to-date and that we had a fancy policy and procedure binder outlining how to handle anything from a bomb threat to a heart attack to fire—all with colour-coded tabs. Then one day there was an earthquake. She fell apart. She started screaming, "Everyone get out! We're all going to die!"

Spoiler alert, we didn't die. We also decided that while she could organize the heck out of us, in an actual emergency she likely wasn't the best person to calmly lead us to safety. Some people are amazing at this. For example, a trained doctor can be in a chaotic emergency room with people screaming, machines beeping, and staff running around and focus in on one patient and calmly deliver the care that's needed. Others melt down when they can't find their car keys or develop an ulcer around final exams.

You will be putting your character under stress. The stress might be the need to save the world from zombies, complete the Kessel Run with a winning time, score in the big game, or declare their love. In many books the situation you're writing about is the most stressful time in a character's life. You may be writing a character like James Bond who's ultimately calm under stress, diffusing a bomb while mixing a martini at the same time, but many characters struggle with the stress as a part of their growth.

Your Turn

- On a scale of one to ten, where one means that your character falls apart under stress, and ten means that they respond to high-stress situations while remaining calm and focusing on what needs to be done, where does your character fall?
- How does your character cope with stress? What do they do when they are stressed?
- How does stress physically manifest itself in your character (headaches, tense shoulders, etc.)?
- How do they deal with situations where they are out of control?

- Prior to the book, what was the most stressful situation your character had dealt with?
- What situations does your character find stressful? For example, some people might cope well in high emergency situations like a fire, but fall apart if someone is emotionally upset.

IMPULSE CONTROL

Impulse Control: **The ability to resist or delay an impulse, drive, or temptation to act. That you do not need to react impulsively, but instead you can weigh your options and the situation to select the best way to respond.**

This is an area many individuals struggle to manage. You may have heard of the famous Stanford marshmallow experiment. Children were given the choice between a small reward of one marshmallow right away or two marshmallow rewards if they were willing to wait for roughly fifteen minutes. Researchers then left the children alone to decide. Some resisted the pull of the marshmallow sitting in front of them, others couldn't. (I'm going on the record. I could have resisted the marshmallow, but if it had been a peanut butter cup there's no way I would have held out.)

In follow-up studies, the children who had been able to delay gratification were reported to have better life outcomes. There's been a further study that seems to show that the outcomes weren't quite as cut and dried as this, and that other factors have a larger impact, but there is still agreement that the ability to delay an impulse is a contributing factor to success.

The ability to put off an immediate response, either to give yourself time to calm down or to weigh an action in the context of a bigger picture goal is key. Individuals who struggle with impulse control can get themselves into all sorts of difficult situations. The impulse could be in any area: anger management, sexual activity, eating, shoplifting, buying items that aren't needed, drinking, or even binging on leftover peanut butter cups post-Halloween for example. (No judgement on that last one.)

While in real life, impulse control is to be applauded, as a writer having characters who struggle with this area provides wonderful opportunities for conflict and trouble. A character who reacts without thinking, who might lash out or leap without looking, is going to give your manuscript some excitement. If you need them to react without thinking you will want to set up that this is a pattern of behaviour, or be able to explain why they normally hold off but this time they don't.

Your Turn

- On a scale of one to ten, where one means that your character is unable to resist an impulse in any area, and ten means that they are able to control those impulses, weigh their decisions before acting and keep their eye on the long-term goal, not just the immediate payoff, where do your characters fall?
- How does your character respond when angry?
- Are there areas where your character struggles more with impulse control than another? For example, can they turn away from warm cookies, but are helpless when they see a sale on shoes?
- Are there particular emotional triggers that set your character off?
- What long-term goal would inspire your character to delay an impulse that they might otherwise give in to?
- Does your character respond the same way to an impulse when they are alone versus when others might see them?
- Most of us struggle more with impulse control in our teen years. This is how we end up in a range of bad situations. Write a journal entry where your character is looking back at a time in their youth when they had poor impulse control. What do they think of that event now? Do they think they would still act in the same way? Are they disappointed in themself?

HAPPINESS

Happiness: **The ability to feel satisfied with your life, to enjoy yourself and your social circle, and to have fun.**

In *The Happiness Project,* author Gretchen Rubin challenged herself to a year-long quest to determine what things impacted her happiness. She presented a question to readers at the start of the book: "What is it that makes you happy?" What she'd discovered is that many of us don't know. Many of us aren't sure what brings us joy and as a result may drift about looking for something. Heck, some aren't even sure what happy feels like for them.

This scale is not about being blissfully happy all the time. No one in real life is a Disney character. (Although if I could get wildlife to sew me clothing and clean my house, I would gladly have an animated life.) For example, you may have someone in your life who's always pursuing something new. They will be happy when they obtain (insert new job, their ideal weight, a car, a vacation, etc.). What we know is that as soon as they get that new job or the jeans that fit like a dream, they will be off wanting something new.

As an author, when considering this trait, ask yourself, is your character generally content? This can be an area where you can create stress or conflict. For instance, having your protagonist interact (or be in a relationship) with someone who is their opposite. If your character has been generally happy in their life, but now that you have increased conflict in the story (their life), how do they respond?

Your Turn

- On a scale of one to ten, where one means that your character is unhappy most of the time and has extreme difficulty finding joy or seeing the bright side of things, and ten means that they know what makes them happy, are able see the positive or find humour even in dark situations, where does your character fall?
- What is fun for your character? What gives them joy?
- What things do they do (often these are small things, pausing for a cup of tea or a hot shower) that they know will pick up their mood?
- Would people describe them as happy? Why or why not?

- Do they rely on others to make them happy?
- When difficult or challenging things happen, do they find humour in it? Can they see the positive? If not, how do they respond when other people react that way?
- If your character is not happy, has this always been the case or did something happen that changed their outlook?

OPTIMISM

Optimism: **The ability to look at the bright side and to maintain a positive attitude, even in the face of difficult times. The direct opposite of someone with high optimism is being a pessimist.**

Optimism has many similarities to happiness, but fundamentally it's an outlook or an approach to life. The belief that things will work out and that life and the world is overall a good place. This is not denial, or living in a dream state, where you can't accept that bad things happen, rather you believe that those bad things can be turned around or will not last.

Some individuals do this in even the darkest situations. Viktor Frankl was a neurologist and psychiatrist who survived the death camps during World War II. Frankl managed to maintain some element of being positive, and finding meaning, and thus a reason to live through what is undoubtedly one of the most brutal situations. He attributed this perspective as part of why he was able to survive with his humanity intact. Following the war, he wrote the book, *Man's Search for Meaning* in which he tried to help others understand this perspective.

I'm fortunate to work with two optimists. They approach problems as opportunities to learn. (Versus my tendency to throw myself overly dramatically across my bed and wail about unfairness.)

The well-respected Mayo Clinic has done research and linked a positive attitude in individuals to health benefits such as a longer life, lower rates of depression, better cardiovascular health and improved resistance to the common cold. In your manuscript, you'll be looking at how your character views the world, which will in part drive their actions.

Your Turn

- On a scale of one to ten, where one means that your character is a complete pessimist who believes the world is a bad place and that there's no point in hoping for better, and ten means that they're an optimist even in difficult or challenging situations, where does your character fall?
- Does your character have a sense of hope about their future?

- What does your character feel about society and humanity? Do they see people as generally good and trustworthy?
- If your character's perspective on this scale has changed (either way), what led to that change?
- The book, *The Secret,* put forward a theory that if you put your hopes and desires out into the world, and if you ask for them, the universe will deliver. What would your character ask for, and would they believe that the universe will deliver?
- Many optimists believe in the power of positive thinking. One common element of this can be positive affirmations, things that we say to ourselves (often into a mirror) and repeat as a way to train our brain to believe them and to replace negative self-talk with this new positive perspective until the brain begins to believe it. Examples of positive affirmations include: I am smart and capable; I am strong, both physically and emotionally; I am a loveable person. What affirmations might your character be trying out? What negative thoughts would they be replacing?

15

EMOTIONAL INTELLIGENCE SUMMARY

EQ is one theory about the elements that form our personality and our approach to life as we interact with the world-at-large and in relationships. For writers, EQ provides a framework for thinking about how your character might behave in any given situation. You can use their areas of strength to help them and their areas of weakness as a way to add to conflict or challenges.

For example, you may be writing a character who is extremely strong on Stress Tolerance, Reality Testing, and Problem Solving. This person is an engineer, who believes that just about anything can be broken down into manageable steps and addressed. However, you as the author may have also determined that she is weak in areas such as Optimism and Interpersonal Relationships. Now we place our engineer character on the deck of a space cruiser. All hell breaks loose. The ship has been attacked by an enemy, pressure has been lost on several decks, people are dying, and the Captain is screaming at our character to do something or all will be lost.

What's working in your engineer's favour is that she will likely remain calm. She'll understand that while the Captain is yelling at her, this isn't personal. Your engineer will be going through possible solutions and evaluating them. On the downside, she'll also be fighting a feeling of hopelessness, that she'd always worried this might happen. Hell, she told the Captain just last week that they didn't have enough transponders to address a direct hit! She doesn't trust that her team of engineering assistants can fix things as well as she can, so she'll be trying to do things herself, wasting additional time. It's also possible that she never trusted the Captain and as a result hasn't been as open about all the supplies she has on-hand. She just knew if she shared what she had, the people in maintenance would requisition it and steal it right from under her.

So, does she save the ship and everyone on it? The situation could go either way, and her strengths and weaknesses will be what pushes and pulls her in different directions. Now, I'm an optimist, so I think she and the crew get their happy ending. Your perspective may be different in which case that bright blip of light you saw last night could have been a shooting star… or their ship exploding.

PART IV

MYERS-BRIGGS PERSONALITY INDICATOR

16

MYERS-BRIGGS PERSONALITY INDICATOR

What is the Myers-Briggs Type Indicator (MBTI)?

You've likely come across the Myers-Briggs test at some point. It's a popular instrument used by schools and organizations to help individuals understand their own behaviour, as well as how others may respond to similar situations in very different ways. It's mainstream enough that many people know and use their profile term (*I'm an INTP*) in social conversations.

This measure was created by Katharine Cook Briggs and her daughter Isabel Briggs Myers and is based on Carl Jung's theory that people experience the world through four principal psychological functions: Sensing, Intuition, Feeling and Thinking. The MBTI is founded on the idea that we all have specific preferences. These preferences impact how we view what happens to us and drives our interests, needs, values and motivations. Jung felt that psychological types are similar to being right- or left-handed, in that you were born with, or develop a preference. He believed these preferences were to some degree hard-wired into us. The MBTI sets up four different scales that result in sixteen possible different types.

In terms of the scientific underpinnings, the MBTI has challenges with validity (some question if it actually measures what it says it measures) and reliability (a person's results can vary depending on when they take the test). Because of these weaknesses, many counsellors use other personality measures, or use the MBTI more as a "getting to know you" tool versus anything that would be considered diagnostic. Despite these challenges it's often used as a way to help individuals understand how they view the world—and for writers it can be a helpful way to explore character development.

Let's explore the four different preference scales.

ATTITUDES: EXTRAVERSION (E) VS INTROVERSION (I)

People often confuse the meanings of these preferences, thinking that extraversion refers to a real "people person" and introversion as someone who is shy and more likely to be a loner. While it may show up in this way, the true meaning is more nuanced.

Extraversion means outward turning. That is the individual gains energy and is recharged by being engaged with the outside world and by action.

Introversion is the opposite, someone who recharges by turning inward—they tend to spend energy to interact and need to have quiet time in order to recharge. This is why you might see someone (*ahem, me*) who can be outgoing and friendly at a conference or social events, but who can find the process tiring and will spend the week after like a hermit to recharge. It isn't that I don't enjoy interacting with others. I do, and I even like public speaking. However, the process of being "out there" drains me. A true extrovert is the opposite, they find the interactions refill their energy stores.

Some ways to see the differences between the two sides include:

- Extraverts are action-oriented, while introverts are thought-oriented.
- Extraverts seek a broad base of knowledge and influence, while introverts seek depth of knowledge and influence.
- Extraverts prefer more frequent interaction with others, while introverts prefer more substantial interaction, but less of it.

Your Turn

Consider your character's attitude to interacting with the world. Would you classify them as an extrovert or an introvert? Some things to consider:

- After a long day, do they seek out social time with friends to unwind (extrovert) or prefer to go home with a glass of wine and Netflix (introvert)?
- Your character has a ton of hobbies that they dip in and out of (extrovert), or do they prefer to have one or two areas that they focus on (introvert)?
- Does your character have a wide range of friends, someone for every occasion (extrovert), or do they have a small band of friends (introvert)?

- Does your character find social events something that they can do at a moment's notice (extrovert), or do they feel like they have to "gear up" for a big night out (introvert)?
- Once you've decided if your main characters are extroverts or introverts score them on a scale of ten, one being not very strongly and ten being very strongly.
- If you want to increase internal conflict for your character, place them in a situation that pushes this scale. That is if they are extroverted, can you limit their interaction with others or have them be unable to act? If they're introverted how can you overload them with people? Consider forcing them to work closely with, or be in a relationship with, someone who is the exact opposite of them. They will almost certainly butt heads.

FUNCTIONS: SENSING (S) VS INTUITION (N)

Jung identified two pairs of psychological functions. Two perceiving functions: sensing and intuition, and two further judging functions: thinking and feeling. He noted that people use all four functions at different times depending on circumstances, but that each of us uses one of them more often (and typically better) than the others.

Sensing and intuition are information-gathering functions. They describe how new information is understood and interpreted. People who prefer **sensing** like information they can see, taste, smell, hear or touch. They like things that are concrete and can be proven. You'll never see someone who scores high in this area who is a big fan of "I just had a hunch" as a plan. People who score high in this area like data and spreadsheets.

Those who prefer **intuition** are less concerned with data and more interested with how new information fits with information they already know. They are typically looking at things in context and attempting to find patterns. They're less concerned with things they get from the five senses and more in understanding what might underlie the data. These are the people who feel comfortable "going with my gut."

In your manuscript, you can increase conflict by either having your character unable to process information in their preferred way or have to rely on someone who uses the opposite approach to make sense of things.

Your Turn

Consider your character's approach to perception. Would you classify it as sensing or intuition?

Some things to consider when making that determination:

- Does your character like to approach problems by thinking about things in terms of data and what they know to be true and then weighing the options (sensing), or do they feel that their gut is a better way to decide (intuition)?
- When your character has a problem, do they back up and think about the big picture (intuition) or do they go about collecting objective data (sensing)?
- Once you've decided whether they lean toward sensing or intuition, score them on a scale of ten, one being not very strongly and ten being very strongly.

- Increase external conflict by having them interact with someone who approaches perception in a different way or increase internal conflict by having them doubt that the way they perceive information is working.

FUNCTIONS: THINKING (T) VS FEELING (F)

Now let's turn to the decision-making, or the judging functions, thinking and feeling. These are used to make decisions based on information received (either through sensing or intuition). Those who lean toward **thinking** tend to decide things by measuring the data and choosing which options seems the most logical. They tend to approach the process in a detached way and like to play by the rules. People who lean toward thinking struggle when they have to work with or interact with people who are inconsistent, whom they see as illogical. They feel the truth is important and will tell it—even if it hurts someone's feelings.

Individuals who prefer a **feeling** approach come to decisions by trying to understand the situation or to see it from another's person's perspective. This can be described as making choices based on values. They'll weigh their options and look for a solution that will achieve the best harmony or they'll help others buy into that resolution. Just as the name would lead you to believe, feelings are important to these people, both their own and anyone else involved.

For clarity, people who identify as thinking are not "better thinkers" than those who identify as feeling. And conversely, people who identify as feeling aren't better at emotions than the thinkers. Both approaches to come to a decision are valid and useful and you can likely start to see where different approaches in different situations will have pros and cons. It's also useful to remember that the MBTI is looking at preferences or the way a person leans, but it's not absolute. You might identify with and lean toward feeling, but that doesn't mean that you aren't capable of approaching a problem with a thinking perspective.

Your Turn

Consider your character's decision-making style, would you classify them as thinking or feeling?

Some things to consider when deciding where your character falls:

- When they need to make a decision, are they likely to weigh all the pros and cons (thinking,) or put an emphasis on how their decision will make other people feel (feeling)?
- Are they annoyed by people who seem illogical (thinking)?

- Is making everyone "buy in" important to them (feeling)?
- If they were buying a car, would your character research all the *Consumer Reports* and ratings (thinking) or would they try a range of cars and see what gives them the best feeling once they sit in it (feeling)?
- Once you've decided if they are thinking or feeling, score them on a scale of ten, one being not very strongly, and ten being very strongly.
- There are likely many opportunities to increase conflict around decision-making points in your book. Can you maximize any of these by contrasting your character's style with those around them or having their preferred approach not work for them in a particular situation?

LIFESTYLE PREFERENCES: JUDGING (J) VS PERCEIVING (P)

Myers and Briggs added another dimension to Jung's model, a judging function, where individuals lean toward either judging or perception. It's about how we approach life, either in a structured way or in more of an open, flexible manner.

People who have a preference toward **judging** like to have things settled. They feel in control when they can take charge of their environment and make choices. They like things to come to a close and "get the job done." They love structure and organization. They want to achieve their goals in a predictable way. The negative view of them is that they could be seen as being too rigid and opinionated.

Those who prefer **perceiving** like to keep things open. For them, too much structure is limiting. They feel in control when they can keep their options open. They are curious and interested in expanding their knowledge and tend to be very tolerant of the idea that others see things differently. The negative view of them could be that they are aimless and drifting.

Your Turn

Consider your character's lifestyle preferences, would you classify them as judging or perceiving?

Some things to consider when deciding where your character falls:

- When planning a trip is your character the type to plan everything and research what they want to see before they go (judging) or do they prefer to just arrive and see what happens (perceiving)?
- If your character is going to join a table at a party would they choose people they know or are certain are similar to them (judging) or would they prefer to just plop down and start talking to new people (perceiving)?
- If going to university, would your character think through schedules, career opportunities and potential earnings before choosing a major (judging) or would they take courses in areas that interest them and decide later what to focus on (perceiving)?

- Once you've decided if they are judging or perceiving, score them on a scale of ten, one being not very strongly and ten being very strongly.
- Look through your manuscript. Are there opportunities to increase conflict by having the character interact with someone who has the opposite approach to them?

THE MBTI TYPE

Once you've measured someone on all of these scales you are given a four-letter code that illustrates which way they lean on the different scales, with sixteen different options available. As you may recall, the MBTI has been criticized in part because of its (lack of) reliability. That is that people may answer the inventory differently at different points in their life or in different environments. It isn't as consistent as psychologists would like, but it *can* still give you a foundation to create characters. When you're creating characters consider not just their dominant type but also how they would have leaned at different times in their life or how they lean in different situations in current time.

The backstory that you created will also have an impact on their score. An individual might have a preference for perceiving, enjoy having things come to them and responding in the moment. However, if you put them through a traumatic event, they may start to lean toward more judging behaviour, deciding that more structure will help them avoid future trauma.

Your Turn

- Consider your character's backstory. How did those events shape which preferences they have on the different scales?
- Will your character's MBTI score be the same at the end of your book?
- The results of the MBTI are sixteen different personality profiles. If you've done the exercises above, you have a pretty good idea of what your character's type is.
- Make a list of the MBTI codes for each of your main characters. Write out their description and consider how well they will work together. Where will they buttress each other's strengths and weaknesses? Where will conflict likely arise?
- If you are writing a series, you'll need to consider how characters change and evolve over several books. To assist you in developing a system to track series details including characters and character details consult Crystal Hunt's book *Strategic Series Author: Plan, write and publish a series to maximize readership & income.*

PART V

CH-CH-CH-CHANGES

17

HOW DO CHARACTERS MOVE THROUGH CHANGE?

David Bowie sang about the need to turn and face the strange changes, but the truth of it is most of us don't like to change. With all due respect to Mr. Bowie, we'd rather *not* turn and face it. Change is uncomfortable and often difficult. It's much easier to talk about what we *would* do than it is to actually do it.

Why is it so hard for people to make change? Especially when they say that they want change?

In *Writing the Breakout Novel:Winning Advice from a Top Agent and His Best-selling Client,* Donald Maass shares one of my favourite exercises. I've done it with every book I've written since I learned about it. He asks writers to indicate what their character wants most and has us write it down. Then he asks us to write down the opposite of that main desire. Then the kicker question, the one that stirs up all sorts of things for us as writers is to answer: *How is it possible for your character to want both of those things at the same time?*

When I first did this exercise in a workshop with Don, I struggled. How is it possible for the character to want the opposite of their primary goal? Won't that make them wishy-washy? Then I realized this is what happens in real life *all the time*. You want to lose weight *and* you want to sit on the sofa watching Netflix while eating a package of Oreos dunked in Baileys Irish Cream. (If you haven't tried it—trust me, it's a thing of beauty.) You want to make partner at your law firm *and* you want to be the best stay-at-home dad the planet has ever known. You want to save the world from interstellar invasion *and* you want to stay on your own planet and not fly in a fighter-jet to face almost certain death from the space lizard people.

In many cases, it isn't that people don't know what they need to do to change. It's not a lack of knowledge or information. There is something else that gets in the way of them moving toward the change they say they want.

As a counsellor, an example I used to share with people who were struggling with a change was to have them picture themselves on a trapeze. It's swinging back and forth, a hundred feet up in the air. You know you can't stay on this trapeze forever… at some point you need to get off. You know that you want to move forward. But what's required is that you let go of what you have (the bar of the trapeze) twist mid-air and have faith that somewhere behind you there is another trapeze that you can grab on to and that you'll swing on that over to the platform.

Talk about a leap of faith.

There's a reason I'm not a circus performer. The idea of letting go of a perfectly safe trapeze bar and spinning around, hundreds of feet in the air while only being "mostly sure" that there will be another trapeze to grab on to makes me nauseated. Change is hard. It's scary. It can mean risking it all, either your actual life, or what might *feel* like life or death.

An example of this can be seen with caged birds. If you capture a bird in the wild and put it into a cage many of them will beat themselves to death on the bars doing anything possible to get out. After a while, if you continue to keep ready access to food and water, most birds begin to like their new home. If you then leave the door open and give them the opportunity to go, they may fly around a bit but will then return to the cage. It becomes a safe place. A place they know. It may not have everything, but it has food, water, and no predators.

Why would we think that we're more evolved than birds? If you put people in a situation where they are at least comfortable, it can be tough to jar them into making some type of change. If you've ever stayed in a ho-hum relationship or dragged yourself to a job you don't like (but heck, you don't hate it, and they pay okay), then you're in a cage too.

18

CHANGE AS A RESULT OF PUSH AND PULL MOTIVATIONS

Counsellors often talk about how change comes about as either a push or a pull; individuals who make a change do so because they are either pushed or pulled to something different than their status quo. For example, imagine that I take you to the top of one of the tallest buildings in New York City. From up there you can see all of Manhattan, from Central Park to the Brooklyn Bridge. I point out that from one corner of the roof the building next door isn't that far away. In fact, the space between the buildings is a mere five feet. Heck, you could get a running start and jump from this building to the next.

Granted you're up 110 stories so if you miss it's going to be a heck of a fall.

Most people won't make that jump. (Although when I share this scenario at high schools there's always an alarming number of teen boys who seem willing to give it a go.) The risk of making that jump, just to say you did, is too high. However, one way to motivate that change is by giving you a push. And I don't mean a hard shove between the shoulder blades. What if I told you that the building we're currently standing on is on fire? The flames have spread to all the stairwells, which means there's no way for us to walk down. The winds are too high for the city to bring in helicopters and the firetruck ladders can't reach us. This means you have a choice—you can either burn to death on the roof of this building or you can make the jump.

In that circumstance, you'll likely remind yourself that you were pretty decent at track back in the day, and then get a good running start to make that leap. That's an example of push motivation. Having life or death stakes is an easy motivation for a reader to understand. If you've set up a situation where the world will blow up (or be taken out by an asteroid, or aliens) unless the character takes on some dangerous act, the reader understands that the immediate threat will make someone do almost anything to save the day—and their life. If your character is in a situation where the heat is continually turned up, making them more and more unable to tolerate their current situation, the more we as readers understand when they make a change.

Pull motivation is the opposite of push. Instead of your current situation being untenable, it is a case that there is something so appealing, so wonderful, so *desirable,* about your goal, that you're willing to take a big risk in order to obtain it. For example, let's go back to the top of that tall building. This time I tell you that on the other roof there is a million-dollar publishing contract that can be yours if you're willing to jump over and grab it. Not all of you, but some, would be willing to take that chance. (Or if you're me, and there's a willing Benedict Cumberbatch on the other roof who is open to a lovely evening at the theatre complete with romance and a cocktail, you better back off because I'm going to give that a go.)

Pull motivations often show up in romance novels. The character has a hint of what it would be like to have love in their life. They might turn away initially, but the appeal of that other person is often enough to pull them into taking a risk on a relationship. This is the scene when they realize that they can't live without that person and we see them dash across town and through an airport to finally declare their love in front of the entire concourse.

When thinking of push/pull, ask yourself if there is a way to make the situation your character is in bad enough that they're willing to risk a lot to make some changes. The other option is to make the goal they are pursuing irresistible. Or you can get all wild and crazy and include both push and pull motivations for your character.

Your Turn

What change is your character resisting? Brainstorm three push reasons and three pull reasons. Use one, or all, to help them through this process.

19

GOAL AND MOTIVATION

This is why it is so important to understand the concepts of goal and motivation. Not just what a character wants, but *why* they want it—what is driving them to obtain it. The craft book *GMC: Goal, Motivation and Conflict: The Building Blocks of Good Fiction* by Debra Dixon explores this in great detail and is a great resource. In particular, it highlights that conflict often comes into play when two characters' goals or motivations are at cross purposes. That is, if you get your goal it means I won't achieve mine.

It's important that your character understands what their goal is. This is the thing, person, or objective that they pursue in the story. They may also have a "need" that they need to resolve. This is often an internal thing. They may not know what emotional growth they need to make, but the goal is the external thing (to win the big game, save the planet, fall in love, find the murderer, etc.). The story is typically resolved when they either get the thing, person, or objective, or they don't.

Motivation is key because as we've established, change is darn hard. The character needs to want to pursue that goal *really* badly in order to keep going, especially when most people would give up. Having a story motivation also drives the reader. If we care why the person achieves their objective, if it means more at a personal level than simply winning, we find ourselves cheering the character on. If the character is successful, then we have a sense of victory because we know it mattered. Even when considering a villainous character, if they have a compelling motivation, we understand them and where they are coming from. It makes the reading experience richer.

Your Turn

- What is an example of a significant change you needed to make in your life? Write a journal entry about that change. What made you want to make it? What were some of the competing interests that kept you from making that change? What kept you going when things got difficult?
- Look at your character's current situation. What would further motivate them to pursue their goal? Asking the question, *What would make this worse?* is a great way to increase the conflict.

- Look at the goal the character is trying to reach,

what would make obtaining that goal even more meaningful for them? How can you make the goal more desirable, and thus irresistible to the character even though you are going to make it difficult for them to obtain? How can it matter *more* if they achieve that goal?

20

NOVELS ARE ABOUT CHANGE

We're talking about change when we use terms like story or character arc. Arc is all about the journey people make from where they are at the start to where they are at the end of the story.

Stories start with a glimpse of the ordinary world. We see the characters in their everyday life when something (the inciting incident) happens that upsets their world and sets them out on a journey. Throughout that journey the character often has to make fundamental changes to how they see the world as they interact with others and themselves. Those changes are what empowers them (or teaches them needed skills) to reach the final goal.

Examples might include:

- A character has to accept the mantle of leadership to guide her people to victory. This may require changes in how she sees responsibility to others or to the greater good, overcoming self-doubt, trusting others, being willing to work as a team or having confidence in her decisions.
- In a romance, a character may have to change their view that the world is a difficult place and that others are out to get them. They will have to break down those internal barriers in order to have a meaningful relationship.
- In a drama, there may be a character who has to tackle addiction in order to move forward in a positive direction. This may require changes in how they cope with challenging issues, the physical aspects of addiction, and who they choose to have in their life.

Often the kind of change that the character needs to make is an emotional or internal change. The challenge for you as a writer is to show that change on the page. The most common way is through internal dialogue where the reader has the opportunity to peek inside a character's mind. However, my task for you is to also look at how you can show that *internal* change in an *external* way.

I've had the good fortune to have a few of my books optioned for film and TV. (Alas, I am still waiting for the opportunity to go full Academy Award diva complete with dark sunglasses and a tiny dog in a purse.) One of the more interesting aspects is seeing how those projects have been adapted for film. Without the use of voice-over (which film people tend to dislike) they must find a way to *show* characters in action that demonstrates what is happening with them internally. You can do this with dialogue, where a character tells another character what is going on with them. In some cases this works, but you run the risk of the dreaded S&T (see the next section for a description of Sitting and Talking).

Your Turn

- Watch the film adaptation of a book you've read. (Yes, I know the book was better.) Look at how the screenwriter adapted the work. What approach did they use to show the character change?
- Take a few scenes from your book that have a lot of internal dialogue. Challenge yourself to come up with a list of ways that you could show the character doing something that would illustrate what they were thinking about a change.

21

SITTING AND TALKING

S&T is the term my go-to early reader (award winning author and writer mentor Joelle Anthony) scribbles in my margin to mean sitting and talking. She loathes sitting and talking scenes. She considers them a cheat. And in fairness, S&T scenes can start clumping up a manuscript before you realize it. You look around the pages and every other chapter people are sitting around kitchen tables, having coffee, or for a wild and crazy variation talking while lying in bed. There's nothing inherently wrong with characters sitting and talking—people do that. The problem is that you're missing an opportunity to see those characters in action while they're talking.

Action has several advantages. It allows you to show change. Action or behaviour can feel more committed than talk. That is, it's easy to talk about how you want to lose weight, but when I see you going to the gym and cooking healthy meals then I'm more likely to believe you. As the cliché goes—talk is cheap.

Action is also visual, allowing the reader to see the scene. Imagine yourself as a screenwriter who doesn't always have the luxury of showing interior thought. People staring at a screen are going to want to see those actors *do something,* so they're constantly looking for how to reveal those emotional changes, motivations and desires.

There is also the opportunity that the type of action the characters are doing or the place where the action takes place can be used to heighten the emotion or tension of a scene. One of my favourite movies is *Love Actually.* In the movie, Emma Thompson realizes that her husband, Alan Rickman is having an affair. She's understandably devastated and she confronts him with what she's learned. This scene *easily* could have become a sitting and talking scene. Emma could have confronted him as they sat around the kitchen table, or in the living room. Instead, the screenwriters made a different choice.

Emma confronts him with the affair as they're waiting to pick up their kids from their Christmas pageant. This heightens the tension as they can't say everything they want, they can't break down into tears, or start screaming, because they're in a very public place. In addition, they're surrounded by the details of family life. There are kids calling out to each other and parents smiling and waving. Alan Rickman's character is suddenly faced with what exactly he's put at-risk with this infidelity. The setting and surroundings makes what was already going to be a high-conflict, high-emotion scene even stronger.

Imagine that you have a character who needs to change a negative outlook and start to be part of their larger community. Things that they might do differently include noticing things happening to other people; seeing the positive instead of being annoyed by things they come across; holding the door open for someone; buying a second cup of coffee for a homeless man instead of ignoring that person. The reader sees those actions and thinks: "Ah! They are starting to care about others." This preps the reader for the character making more significant life changes as the book evolves.

Another example: You may have a married couple who have been trying to start a family for some time and not having any luck. They haven't talked about it, but at this point, the wife wants to have infertility testing. Instead of them talking about this over dinner, consider having them hold the discussion while doing some home renovations.

As any couple can tell you, if you want to see how you'll work out long-term as a couple, do a construction project together. There's the opportunity for conflict about how to get wallpaper off that is really a conversational placeholder until we can talk about the "real" issue, the infertility. If the husband talks about not trying to force anything, and just let things take time, she may have a response to that idea that has little to do with wallpaper removal. The idea of renovating a house to make it a home also can play into the desire to have a family to fill that home. There's a lot of room for you as the writer to weave in issues related to the theme and to increase the conflict, not to mention to have a lot of visually interesting things for the reader to see and the character to interact with as that conversation happens.

Your Turn

- What change does your character need to make over the course of the story?
- How will this change impact how they see the world, see others, and themself?
- How many sitting and talking (S&T) scenes do you have in your book? Is there a way to put those characters into action instead? They might still have some of the same dialogue, but how can the action enhance the scene?

22

STAGES OF CHANGE

When creating meaningful and believable change in your character it can be useful to understand how change occurs in real people. When I worked as a counsellor, I learned the stages of change and what types of things would motivate people from one stage to another. The goal was always to meet individuals where they were at the moment. Too often we try to encourage people to change with brute force. We think if they only knew why they shouldn't continue with whatever behaviour they are demonstrating, or if they knew alternatives then, *of course,* they would make a change. Then we're frustrated when this doesn't work.

The Transtheoretical Model of Change was introduced by James Prochaska in 1982. It combines a number of theories of change into a five-stage model including: Pre-Contemplation, Contemplation, Preparation, Action and Maintenance.

It was created to help therapists understand how change happens, where a person is in the stages of change, and what to do to help move them through the stages. It was focused on changes such as weight loss, quitting smoking and increasing fitness, but it works and has been applied to a range of changes including coping with chronic pain. As a writer, you can use the model to help you understand where your character might be in the course of the novel and then create realistic situations that help to move them from one stage to another.

Let's go through the five stages and use the idea of quitting smoking as a change that a person is trying to make so that you can see the stages in action. We'll create a character, Derek, who has a two-pack-a-day smoking habit as an example.

STAGE ONE: PRE-CONTEMPLATION

At the pre-contemplation stage the individual has no intent to change. They are unaware, or under-aware, of their problem(s.) Someone at this stage may feel coerced to change. If you could be inside their head, they would have thoughts like: *"What problem? The only problem I have is people who keep telling me I have a problem."*

Our character Derek would blow smoke rings while telling you that he feels great. Smoking doesn't bother him at all. And did you know, his grandmother smoked three packs a day and she lived to be 105? And she liked to jog while she smoked. Derek would have a complicated theory on how the science around the dangers of smoking was some kind of fake news brought about by an evil cabal who hates tobacco farmers. Alternately he might make flippant comments like: *"Yeah, smoking is bad for you, but everyone's gotta die of something."*

People at a pre-contemplative stage will not change. They will have every reason and excuse to *not* alter what they do. If you want to encourage someone at this stage to make a change you will fail if you go at them trying to explain why they must do something differently. You can't get them to change, but hopefully you can move them forward in the stages which will eventually lead to the actual switch in behaviour. We'll talk about what might help with that later.

Your Turn

- If your character is at a pre-contemplation stage, what story or narrative do they tell themself that makes them downplay or ignore the problem?
- Are there other characters in your manuscript who recognize there is a problem? How have they tried to raise this issue with your character? How did this go over?

STAGE TWO: CONTEMPLATION

At this stage, the individual is aware a problem exists. However, they have no commitment to change, or they may talk about how they will change someday in the future with no definite plan. If you were inside this individual's head, they would be saying something like: *"Okay...there's a small problem and one of these days I'm going to do something about it."*

Our character Derek would be making comments like: "Yeah, yeah, I know smoking is bad for you, and I'm totally planning to quit once (insert excuse here—my wife gets pregnant, I'm done with exams, I turn forty, this stressful situation with my ageing parents is resolved, etc.).

One common behaviour in this stage is weighing the pros of the problem and cons of the solution. By doing this the person who needs to make a change can acknowledge the problem but justify their lack of action. For example, our character Derek would have pros like: smoking relaxes me, smoking is the one way that I actually take a break during the day, it's such a social thing, it looks so retro and vintage. He would also talk about the cons of quitting: I'm going to gain weight if I stop smoking, my smoker friends will feel bad that I'm not hanging out with them anymore, the only time I get outside of the office during the day is on my smoke break.

Your Turn

- What excuses does your character have for not changing at this time?
- What are the pros of the character staying in their current life without making a change?
- What are the cons of the character making a change?

STAGE THREE: PREPARATION

At long last, we start seeing some movement to change. This stage combines intention with behaviour, but at this point it is more about planning than doing anything. You'll see individuals gathering information and resources. Keep in mind just because they have a plan, it may not be a good plan. For instance a person might say they need to lose weight but their plan is to eat nothing but wheat crackers and fruit until they are thin. Inside the head of someone who is at this stage are thoughts like: *"I need to figure out how to tackle this problem. I need a plan. This is what I am going to do."*

Our character Derek is talking to people about quitting smoking and exploring what worked for them. He has perhaps stopped in the aisle of the grocery store that sells Nicorette gum and checked out the price. He's paying attention to how many times a day he takes a smoke break and is noticing ads on the subway for hypnosis programs.

He wonders if that might work. It's possible he's even set a date—that on his birthday he's going to quit.

One of the key indicators a person is in this stage is that they are noticing things. Have you ever had the experience that you buy a new car, a Kia for example, and suddenly you notice there are Kias *everywhere*? It seems like you pass at least one a day on your drive and last time you were at the grocery there were three in the lot, one even the same colour as yours!

Another example is someone who just found out they're pregnant. When they look around it seems like there's been an invasion of other pregnant women and everyone has a baby. There are babies and baby goods everywhere they look. There's actually a term for it, Baader-Meinhof Phenomenon, otherwise known as the frequency illusion or recency illusion. This happens because your brain is rather excited about this new thing and selective attention begins to occur. Your subconscious is fired up and is sending messages that "I'm going to go look for that thing," even though you won't be consciously thinking about it.

As a writer, you can show that a character is in this stage by having them notice what is going on around them in a way that may not have done before. They'll be collecting information about what might help them to make a change and beginning to put the pieces in place to make it happen. As mentioned above, the plan they come up with may not be a great plan. And unless you're writing a short story, their plan is likely going to have some significant hiccups and challenges before they have success.

In many stories there is a mentor character. (Let's give a shout out to all the bearded old white dudes like Dumbledore, Gandalf, and Obi-Wan Kenobi who have filled this role for years). Their purpose in the story is to assist the main character with what they need to learn and grow. Fundamentally they help with the preparation. For example, Derek may have a co-worker or friend who quit years ago who is around to offer advice and support.

Mentor characters are there to educate not only the protagonist, but the reader as well. It's often through the teachings of the mentor that the reader understands the stakes, just how hard it will be to have success, and what's going to be required to obtain this knowledge. Mentors are often a character that allows the writer to slip in details of backstory and history. *"There has been trouble with the Alciaan race since the rebellion two hundred years ago. People initially thought that the Senate guards would be able to do away with them in no time, but strange things began to happen. Rumours started that the Alciaans were using magic." Etc.*

Your Turn

- In your manuscript what kinds of resources or information does your character need to make a plan? Where will they go to find these things?
- What things can you place into the setting and surroundings that your character could begin to notice?
- Is there a character in your story who can serve in

the mentorship role and help your protagonist? And keep in mind if you have a wiser, more capable mentor character you're going to have to create a reason that this mentor can't solve the problem themselves. (Your inner serial killer strikes yet again.)

STAGE FOUR: ACTION

All this time you've been waiting for it and finally it's here—the individual is *doing* something. At this stage people modify their behaviour, experiences, or environment in order to overcome the problem. This is often the first time the outside world may notice that an individual is changing. This stage is often exciting for the person as they are putting those plans into action. Anyone who has been planning anything (a vacation, a dinner out, a house renovation) knows that when you get to take the first steps it's a relief, a bit anxiety-producing at times, and thrilling—all in one go. If you were inside someone's head at this stage, you'd hear thoughts like: *"Watch this!"* or *"Here I go!"*

Derek may mark his move into being a non-smoker with some kind of ritual. He may toss his last pack of cigarettes into a paper shredder, or he may linger after grinding out the butt of his last cigarette. On the page, we'd see him attaching a non-smoking patch, going to a hypnosis appointment or walking right past the display of cigarettes at the store. When Derek's co-workers pause at his desk and ask if he wants to join them for a cigarette break, he'll pat his breast pocket, remember, and then turn down their offer.

Initial steps of action tend to be positive. We've been building up to this change, convincing ourselves that we really want it. It feels good to *do* something toward our goal. If you've ever decided to eat healthier and become more fit this is the glorious stage where you come back from the gym and feel smug and proud of yourself for going (on a Monday morning no less!). Then you clean out all of your cupboards and fridge tossing the Oreos, Pringles and triple crème brie cheese into the trash. This is the moment in the road trip where you back out of the driveway, crank on the travel playlist you made just for this moment and have that glorious sense of going somewhere.

Later stages of action are often more difficult. You've started to do things differently, but different is hard. In the examples above, this is the moment where your alarm goes off two weeks later and you really, really, *really* don't want to get up to go to the gym. What you want is to sleep for another forty minutes. Or you're at the restaurant and you know you should have the baked salmon with salad (dressing on the side please), but the item on the menu that is calling your name is the triple cheese and Italian sausage lasagna.

If you're on the road trip, this is where you've been sitting in bumper-to-bumper traffic for at least thirty minutes and are fuming about how everyone is driving like idiots. It's the moment when you realize that you forgot some key item that you really wanted to bring and you're officially too far from home to easily go back and get it.

The final stage below deals with how people cope with those difficulties, but it's important to mention here so you know that it isn't always going to be smooth sailing when making a change. Either in real life or in fiction.

Your Turn

- Does your character have any kind of ritual to mark the fact they are embarking on a change? Examples might be a makeover, new clothing, holding some kind of ceremony, telling others, cleaning the house, destroying something that symbolizes what they are changing, etc.
- What are the positive experiences that your character has at the start of a new change?
- As the change continues, what are the challenges that the character faces that make them wonder why in the world they thought this decision was a good idea?
- How do the people around them respond to this change? Are they supportive?

STAGE FIVE: MAINTENANCE

Change is rarely a static thing, it's often dynamic. For example, if your goal is to be healthier including eating better and exercising more, you never reach a point where you're fit and don't have to think about it again. It is a constant process, involving deciding over and over about what you will eat and to go to the gym. And anyone who has ever decided to put their health as a priority knows, it is all too easy to slip into old habits. This is why the fitness industry is a billion-dollar business, because it's a never-ending process and many of us struggle. In this stage an individual works to prevent relapse and consolidate gains to keep the change in process.

If you were inside the head of the person at this stage, they would be having thoughts like: *"Okay so I ate the cake, so what? Tomorrow I'll hit the gym again. It's no big deal."* Or *"I know I said I would trust my partner more so I'm not going to go through their phone and check their text messages. Not only do I not want them to think I have to check, but I also don't want to be the kind of person who does that."* This stage is about picking yourself back up if there's any kind of relapse in desired behaviour, or about reminding yourself of what you are gaining by continuing with this change.

Our friend Derek is likely struggling. He may be dreaming about smoking or there may have been that time after a few beers when having a smoke was irresistible, even though his mouth tasted like an ash tray when he woke up the next morning. We might see Derek, trying to quit, failing and then quitting again.

This stage plays a large role in many stories as it is here where the character struggles with their commitment to move forward. For example, you may structure your story where the inciting incident is the character deciding to make a change. They make a plan and put it into place, but the second and third acts are all about how well they do at continuing with this change when the going gets rough.

For instance, if you're writing a book about a character who has an addiction the inciting incident may be that social services comes to take the children out of the home. The character enters a rehab facility. The bulk of the book is their effort to get and stay sober. Most likely there will be a dark moment around the ¾ point of the story where they have a significant relapse (perhaps right before a court appointment about custody of the kids—when in doubt always go with making things worse for your character). The end of the book will either be the character getting sober again and making some kind of change that shows their commitment to this act (happy story) or they will spiral back into addiction (sad story).

However, there is no clear or easy way to map the Stages of Change to the stages or turning points in a story. You could also write a story about a character who is an addict, but the inciting incident is them losing their kids, but being unwilling or unable to recognize that they have a problem. The first half of the book may be all about them in the early first stages of change, pre-contemplation and contemplation. It may be that it isn't until the climax of the book when they finally decide that they are willing to make a change. We see them take action in the final scene, but the book will never show the reader how they do in those final stages.

Your Turn

- What are the things that your character needs to do to show they are continuing to make a positive change?
- What internal challenges will your character face when making a change?
- What external challenges will your character face when making a change?
- Will your character "relapse" into past behaviour? What is the final thing that pushes them over into this?

- How does your character react when they relapse into old behaviours?
- How do people around them react when your character relapses?
- What makes your character finally triumph?

23

WHAT MOVES PEOPLE THROUGH THE STAGES OF CHANGE?

When the Stages of Change are being used by counsellors, we know there are specific motivational tasks that can assist someone in moving to the next level.

At the Pre-Contemplation stage our goal is to raise doubt, to increase the perception of the problems and risks of what they are doing. Remember, at this stage the person doesn't think there is a problem, so we want to help them gain awareness that one might be there.

At the Contemplation stage we are trying to tip the balance. The person has started to acknowledge that there's a problem, but they're not ready to commit to a change. Our goal is to continue to raise awareness of reasons for change and what is at-risk if they don't. We want to reinforce the idea that we believe they can change and move forward.

When an individual is in the Planning stage the best way to assist them is to support their efforts to make a plan. This might include raising other options and helping them evaluate the pros and cons of the options under consideration.

During the Action stage a counsellor is there to cheer the individual on toward taking actual steps. This might include assisting them with specific tasks or simply providing emotional support. Often during this stage, we also warn the individual that there will be some bumps ahead but reassure them we know they're going to handle them.

In the final stage, Maintenance, we review progress to ensure the individual can recognize how far they've come and, as needed, review the reasons for change to keep their motivation high. If the individual is struggling, there may be some benefits to reviewing the plan and seeing if there are any other actions or supports that should be in place to help when things are difficult.

So, what types of specific things might be happening that you can use in a manuscript?

- Consciousness Raising
- Dramatic Relief
- Environmental Re-Evaluation
- Self Re-Evaluation
- Self-Liberation
- Reinforcement Management

CONSCIOUSNESS RAISING

This involves increased awareness and information about the causes, consequences, and cures for a particular problem.

What this might look like in a manuscript

- The stakes are raised by showing how their behaviour could harm them. For example, if someone needs to eat better or be more fit, they may have a heart attack or other life-threatening health issue.
- The character may interact with or observe someone who has the same problem and see how it worked out (or not) for them. This the "ghost of future Christmas" coming to warn the character of what things will look like if they don't change.

- A positive spin on this involves the character interacting with or observing someone free of this problem and having the realization, "Wow, it would be amazing to live like that."
- You'll occasionally see this done in a montage type scene where the character has moment-after-moment where their problem is front and centre.
- Another character may confront them about their behaviour.
- Your character may stumble across, or have another character bring to their attention, a possible solution to their problem. This can be effective if the character has convinced themselves that this is a problem where nothing can be done, and they must simply learn how to live with it.

Your Turn

- What people or events around your character make them aware that they have a problem?
- Is there another character in the story who can be an example to your protagonist about what will happen to them if they do (or don't) change?

DRAMATIC RELIEF

One thing we know is that strong emotions like passion, fear, and anger often drive change. I can provide a personal example of this. As a child, my dad was a smoker. At that time in our house the routine was that Mom was the one who got me up and moving in the mornings and in the evenings, Dad would do the bedtime routine, complete with a story and a goodnight kiss.

One day I declared that I no longer wanted the story and goodnight kiss. My dad inquired if I felt I was simply too old. Apparently, I looked at him with my wide eyes and said: *We saw a video in school about the dangers of smoking, so I know that you're going to die. I just don't want to love you as much as I do now.* Then I turned around with a dramatic sad sigh and trudged off to bed—no doubt with his still beating heart that I ripped from his chest in my tiny little hand.

He quit smoking.

I don't want to imply it was easy, but arousing strong emotion about a behaviour, and letting someone know that emotion could be relieved, can lead to changing that behaviour. This is why someone who has resisted being fit might suddenly start going to the gym if they have a significant health scare. Or someone who has been taking a relationship for granted might have a change-of-heart if they believe someone is trying to woo their partner away.

What this might look like in a manuscript

- **A dramatic event may be the inciting event in your story**. This could include a near-death experience, a death, an accident, a moment of rage or abject terror that forces your character to stop and take stock of where their life is and determine if they want to continue on course.
- **A less dramatic event, but with an emotional impact**. Sometimes the event itself isn't that dramatic but it causes a moment in which the character is hit emotionally. For example, a character who attends a friend's wedding, looks around and realizes that all of their old university friends are married. Suddenly, in the middle of the reception, all they see are people all matched up, happy couples, families mugging for the camera and it hits them—they are alone. The rest of the story is their pursuit of love. Another character might be at work with a demanding and dismissive boss. However, this morning the homeless guy outside the coffee shop makes a

flippant comment about how they would never put up with that kind of treatment and the character is shocked to realize that while he (or she) has a job and the financial success that goes with that, they don't have any freedom or joy in their day-to-day life and quit on the spot.
- **A relationship shake-up**. There are times in our lives when the push for change comes from an external source. Someone in our life declares that they can no longer put up with our drinking and walks out the door. Or a person that we love and admire tells us a hard truth about ourselves that perhaps we've been trying to deny. This might come out in an argument or it might be done in a loving way, but the emotion of what is communicated has an equally large impact on the character.

Don't be afraid to take your character to these places. Remember, change happens with strong emotion. Not irritation or frustration, but rage or being livid. You have to be willing to push your characters to have them feel those emotions that are on the ragged edge.

Your Turn

- What strong emotion is most difficult for your character to handle?

- Is there someone who has the most impact on them (a child, best friend, parent) whose opinion would garner a strong emotional reaction?

ENVIRONMENTAL RE-EVALUATION

This is the realization of how one's behaviour affects one's environment and how changing would impact that environment. A counsellor who is trying to help someone with this area has the individual consider their surroundings (including the people in it) and imagine how it might be different if they were to address the problem.

The space around us is often a reflection of how we are feeling emotionally and who we are as people. This doesn't mean that you have to have a perfectly clean house to be happy, but if your home is in chaos it might indicate that you have some level of emotional chaos going on as well. An individual who has a home where they can tell if a vase is a quarter-of-an-inch out of place and who picks up and immediately washes and puts away an empty glass as soon as you put it down tends to indicate that the individual living there has a need for control.

Consider the first time that you went over to the home of a person you were dating. You likely looked around to see what you could tell about them from their space. What kinds of books did they have on their shelves? (Or did they have no books at all? Oh, the horror!) Was their place casual or formal? Creepy paintings of sad clowns on the wall, or black and white nature photographs? When we look around their space, we're looking for clues to better understand them.

A counsellor may also look at how a person presents themselves. Once we're old enough to choose our own clothing we tend to select items that reflect the image that we want to portray. This is why teens often try out different looks as they determine who they might be—sporty, or really casual, or all business, or in a way that shows that status is important to them. We dress for ourselves, but also for others. Clothing is a walking billboard that we use to communicate to those around us who we are and who we want to be.

Let's look at some examples to understand how environmental re-evaluation might work. Imagine that a person is considering becoming more fit. The individual might imagine how it would feel to go up the stairs and not feel winded. Or to be able to join a group of friends who are going hiking up a mountain. They might picture themselves buying new clothing and liking how they look.

An individual going through a divorce may imagine the home that they'll have on their own. They picture it without the fighting and strife that may have been common in their marriage. The individual can decorate it any way they want, invite anyone over they want, watch whatever they want on the TV without a disapproving partner saying, "Are you *really* going to watch that?"

What this might look like in a manuscript

Your character is looking around and noticing things in their environment. They may either be growing annoyed with their current status quo or becoming inspired by what they see others doing.

As a writer this allows you to use setting to its maximum advantage. How does the space around the person reflect their current state or who they would like to be in the future? For example, a well-known trope is having a character who has been down in the dumps look around. They're wearing sweatpants and if they're honest, they don't even know how many days in a row they've had them on. Their hair isn't washed and they're pretty sure the stain on their shirt is dried cereal. The apartment is a mess! Empty, greasy pizza boxes by the door, dishes in the sink, one sock draped across a lamp and a layer of dust that is approaching blanket-like levels on everything.

Suddenly they've had it! Up next there's the scene where they take a shower, scour the house, and the reader sees them dumping out bags of trash and buying flowers for the table. It cues the reader that there's been a change.

There's a common writing prompt that has you imagining opening your character's fridge (or purse, or bedroom) and seeing what's inside. It's the idea of how the things around a character may tell us something about them. A person whose fridge is full of tofu, Whole Foods salads in tidy recyclable tubs, coconut water and a bag of ground flax seed seems different to us than a character whose fridge contains Chinese take-out and a single bottle of ketchup.

If you enjoy film, pay attention to costumes. A huge effort is made with costumes to show the audience more about the character and to reflect tone and feel. For example, in the start of *Star Wars* (Episode 4) we see Luke Skywalker on Tatooine. He's wearing a simple outfit (after all he's a farmer) in neutral colours. It's not shabby, but it's clearly well-worn and in no way stands out. At the end of the film he's in a great hall of chrome and glass striding forward to get a medal for bravery from Princess Leia. Luke's wearing an outfit that looks like the military man he's become. His clothing (and the setting) reflects the change in him.

Your Turn

- Look around your character's space, what does that space say about them? If you're wanting to show that they're making a change, what about their space changes?
- Now do the same with what they're wearing. What clothing does your character wear and what does their style say about them? Are they happy with what they're communicating, or would they wear something different if they felt confident to do so?

SELF RE-EVALUATION

This refers to the visualization of your self-image free from a particular problem. It's the idea that an individual can imagine what their life may be like, and how they would view themselves, if they were able to address their problem.

You've likely heard of (or practice) the theory of positive thinking. It's more than thinking happy thoughts. Research shows that negative thoughts have an impact on the brain. This comes about in part as a survival technique. If you're walking through the woods and come across an angry bear, your brain registers a negative emotion (terror) and then responds by telling you to run! Part of what your brain does in this moment is narrow its focus. It eliminates your ability to see options because if you're facing a bear you don't have time to go through all those options. If you're in a negative frame of mind it can be hard to see opportunities. Research has shown that people who experience positive emotions identify and see more opportunities and possibilities.

Earlier we talked about the differences between push and pull when discussing motivation; self re-evaluation is an area where pull is at play. In this state, the individual is thinking about how they would feel if they were able to address this issue and make the change. They're expressing what they want.

This type of support only works once the individual has acknowledged that they have a problem and want to make a change, such as between the contemplation and planning stage. One thing that can help move the planning forward is imagining how great it will be once you're through the difficult part of the change. It can help keep you motivated as you work through those challenges of the transition. However, if someone is still in pre-contemplation stage, they don't believe there is a problem, thus there is no reason for them to make any changes.

What this might look like in a manuscript

One way that counsellors help with this is by having clients practice visualization. For writers, what you will need to do is show that the character is imagining their life differently. This might be done through internal dialogue or by having them discuss the impact of making that change with another trusted character.

Your Turn

- If your character was to have a dream about the life they would like to have, what would it look like?
- Is there someone around your character who could assist them in imagining their life in a new way?

SELF-LIBERATION

This includes both the belief that you can change as well as the commitment and recommitment to act on that belief. A character at this stage is likely in the Action or Maintenance stage. They're either in the process of putting changes into place or are monitoring their progress.

In order to offer this kind of support the counsellor is reinforcing positive statements, and if the individual is expressing negative thoughts then they are helping the individual to reframe those thoughts. For example: *I can't do this*, versus, *I don't know how to do this particular task, but I can learn.* From: *I've never been able to lose weight,* to *I've learned some good nutrition habits and I can lose weight this time.*

We know that if people have only one choice that their motivation to change is lower than if they have two or more choices. When people feel they have autonomy to choose a direction and way forward then they are more committed to the process. This is why if someone is choosing a fitness plan for example, it is better to offer suggestions and choices such as: you could start with walking, or there's a yoga class, or you might start by meeting with a trainer. An individual who feels they are selecting a way forward that is best-suited to them is more likely to be successful.

What this might look like in a manuscript

You can show a character in this stage through internal thinking where the reader sees that they are beginning to believe they will be successful. Now you might still pull the rug out from under them during a dark night of the soul moment, but at least at one point in the change they have the belief that they will make it. This is also where we may see a character trying out different ways to reach their goal as they attempt to find the way that's going to work the best for them.

Your Turn

- What options does your character have when making a change?
- Write down negative things that your characters say about themselves. How could they start to spin these toward the positive?

REINFORCEMENT MANAGEMENT

This support occurs during the Maintenance stage. It involves the systematic use of reinforcements and punishments for taking steps in a particular direction. Successful self-changers rely much more on reinforcement than on punishment. That is, carrots tend to work better than sticks.

Individuals who are considering making a change do best to have regular check-ins once they have started to alter their behaviour and opportunities to reward themselves along the way. This is why at The Creative Academy we encourage people to take part in regular retreats and accountability sessions where they break their bigger goals into smaller pieces.

For example, instead of having the goal of "finish my 100k manuscript" we'll encourage them to commit to write for thirty minutes a day. And, when a writer hits a goal, like writing every day for 30 days, we celebrate with them. Those mini-celebrations encourage people to keep going. A large change is difficult and typically takes time. Being rewarded along the way not only ensures that someone keeps trying, the task feels more achievable, (writing a full book is hard, writing a chapter is more doable) and they are also more likely to keep going, even if they falter along the way. This is why many change groups (Weight Watchers, AA, etc.) involve an element of regular check-ins where people can be encouraged and reinforced with the change they're making.

This doesn't mean that there isn't some space for there to be a stick in addition to the carrot, but in general, a positive approach will work better.

What this might look like in a manuscript

Consider what good things (rewards) your character can get to help keep them on-track along the way to reaching their goal. Not only will this keep your character motivated, but it will also signal to the reader that the character is moving in the right direction. The reader will cheer the character on and be happy that they got some reward for their efforts.

Your Turn

- What carrots would be meaningful for your characters to motivate them to keep going?

- What sticks would be meaningful for your characters to get them motivated?
- Are these sticks or carrots coming from inside your characters (as a result of self-reflection and evaluation), or are they coming from an external source?

THE IMPACT OF OTHERS

So far, our discussion about change has focused on how the individual moves through the various stages of change and what will help them. However, change rarely happens in a vacuum. It impacts the people around us.

It's important to consider how other people around your character feel about them making that change. The first thing to look at is who is supporting their decision. It might be the people closest to them, but a helping hand might come from an unexpected source, too. At times the people who may be more distant in our life, or even people we've seen as antagonistic, may be the ones who step-up when we need them.

Counsellors work with individuals to identify who in their life might be a support as they move through any kind of transition. We have them communicate with that person and enlist their help.

What this might look like in a manuscript

From a writer's point of view, you'll consider who supports your character. You may already have a mentor in place, a Dumbledore or an Obi-Wan, who's there to assist your character in learning what they need to know to ultimately succeed. Even if there isn't a formal mentor, you'll likely have a character who is the best friend or partner who provides guidance and support to your character and acts as a sounding board.

Keep in mind that whomever supports your character must either a) not be as capable as your character to solve the problem or b) must be unable for some reason to step into the breach and solve the problem. This is why many mentor characters meet with an unfortunate end in stories. They are the one better-equipped to deal with problems and thus rather than wait for your character to step up, learn, and change so they can solve things, the reader wonders why this better qualified character doesn't handle things.

But not all support is positive. Why do some people (who in theory love you) sometimes try to sabotage you when you're making a positive change? For example, you may declare that you are going to eat healthier. Your partner or good friend initially may be very supportive, but as you lose weight they may start to change. Suddenly they're encouraging you to order dessert: *"Oh, come on, it's just some crème brûlée, we'll share it, you don't want to be no-fun."* Or perhaps you come home, and someone has made cookies; the smell of those melty chocolate chips wafting through the whole house. *"Don't you want just one? I made them for you."*

Or perhaps it is about writing. You've been in a critique group for years that is supportive and a great place to go and vent. Then you decide it's time to stop talking about writing a book and instead do it. You start turning out pages, going to conferences and sending your work out. People who might have encouraged your ideas may suddenly come up with reasons why that conference is a waste of your time or how they heard no one makes any real money with writing.

What about your change threatens them? It could be that if you change it forces them to consider some difficult options. First off, that perhaps they should be making changes of their own. If we're in it together then we're a team. But if you are doing something different it highlights that perhaps I should be making changes, too. If I feel that change is impossible, but you're demonstrating by your own efforts that it's hard, but doable, then I have to confront my own efforts. (Or lack of effort.)

Another possible reason that someone might sabotage you is that your change impacts their narrative. For example: *You're the pretty one. I'm the smart one. If you get a Masters degree and become pretty* ***and*** *smart where does that leave me?* Just as we all have a story about ourselves, a mythology, so do the people around us. We each have roles that we play in our own story, but also in the stories of the people around us.

For example, maybe we've been friends since childhood where we met in art class. I was the responsible one and you were the one who was always a bit of a flake. I gave up art for a "real job," got married and had kids (2.5 of them, one boy one girl and also an adorable black lab puppy.) You always flitted between toxic relationships and more than once you ended up sleeping in my (well-appointed) guest room after a horrid break-up. I would never tell you to your face, but the truth is sometimes I feel bad for you.

Then you decide to get your act together and take your art seriously. You commit to your work. You decide that while relationships are great, you're going to focus on yourself. You start to have success with your art (books, painting, sculpture). You're traveling around the world, spending weeks in Paris. You never have Cheerios spilled all over your back seat. You don't live in the boring suburbs. You're having sex with guys who don't leave their toe-nail clippings on the bathroom floor or constantly complain that his mother makes roasted chicken better.

Wait a minute. Your life isn't supposed to be better than mine! I'm supposed to feel slightly bad for you while feeling that I'm just a tiny bit superior. What if I was the one who did it wrong by getting married young? What if the story I told myself about how playing it safe was the right thing to do was incorrect and if I'd taken more chances, I could be living my dream life making art? If this is the situation, I might start to erode your change, second-guess your decisions, and attempt to convince you to do something else.

Your Turn

- What change(s) does your character need to make over the course of the story? Distill this down to no more than three sentences.
- If the change is internal, how do you plan to show this externally? That is, if they need to learn to trust others, what will this look like? What will they say or do that shows the outside world that they are trusting?
- What do the people around your character think of this change? Are they supportive or do they sabotage your character? What does their support look like? If they aren't helpful, what are they doing and why are they doing it?
- What motivates your character to make this change? What motivates them not to change? They will likely have motivations on both sides, remember they want to write a book, but they also want to binge-watch that new show.
- How does your character's physical space reflect their internal status? Does this change over the course of the book?
- What does your character gain from a change? How would their life be better?
- What does your character give up if they make this change?
- Does your character fail in their effort to make the change?

- How does your character respond to the failure? Do they have a system of rewards or punishments to keep them going? If you have a moment in the book when it seems like all is lost and the character is teetering on the brink of giving up, what gives them hope to try one more time?
- How do others around your character respond to failure?

24

BACKSTORY AND CHANGE: BRINGING IT TOGETHER

This book has explored the importance of a character's backstory. How the events that happened in the past shaped who they are today, who they are at the start of your book and perhaps more importantly how they will react when you put them under pressure. Hopefully I've convinced you that knowing backstory is important so that you're able to get a better point of view and deeper understanding of where your character is coming from.

We explored how that backstory impacted the development of the character's personality. Emotional Intelligence and the Myers-Briggs are both frameworks to help you understand a character's strengths and weaknesses. They should provide you with some ideas on instinctive character responses to situations and help you identify areas where they need to grow. You can set up situations where conflict between characters (and also internal conflict) will be organic and almost certainly explosive. Which, while less than ideal in real life, is great for fiction!

Lastly, we explored how individuals make change. Our characters grow and change over the course of the book. They are confronted with difficult situations from rogue dragons to aliens to serial killers that must be stopped. They fall in love, out of love, and into bed. Their growth is often what leads them to achieving their story goal, or if they fail to grow this might lead them to tragedy. As a writer, understanding how people move through change allows you to show it on the page in a three-dimensional and believable way.

Overall, the important take-away from this book is that **it's not what happens to your character that matters—it's the narrative that they tell themselves about those events.** The meanings they put onto things and how that history shapes their current personality, how they respond to current events and how they move through the change process.

Taking time to explore your character's personality allows you to create richer characters that feel real and three dimensional to the reader.

Your Turn

Exercise 1: Leave a review

I hope you found this book helpful. I'd be forever grateful if you took a moment right now to post a quick review wherever you bought your copy, and on Goodreads and / or BookBub if you have accounts there.

Your review will help other writers find the book.

It also helps me know what you found most helpful. This book is part of a series and your feedback will ensure our next books give you more of what you liked–so if you include of something you loved or found helpful in your reviews we'll see it and take note!

Exercise 2: Share with a friend

The only thing better than writing and reading books is sharing books with friends. If you know other writers who could use help upping their backstory game, please let them know you enjoyed this one and found it helpful in developing your characters.

Exercise 3: Join our Mighty Network of Writers

Having a community who understand what you're going through as a writer makes all the difference between getting stuck or getting done.

Join our fabulous free community at **https://creativeacademyforwriters.com/join-us** and get access to a whole whack of resources and support.

Exercise 4: Check out the other books in the Creative Academy Guides for Writers series

It's always sad when you come to the end of a book. But put away your Kleenex. We've got more books to help you along your writer journey. If you visit our books page at **creativeacademyforwriters.com/books** and get on our mailing list we'll let you know every time we add a new book to the series so you don't miss out!

More Creative Academy Guides for Writers

We've got a whole series of books to help you along your writing and publishing journey.

Available in eBook & print!

Scrappy Rough Draft by Donna Barker
Build Better Characters by Eileen Cook
Strategic Series Author by Crystal Hunt
Create Story Conflict by Eileen Cook
Full Time Author by Eileen Cook and Crystal Hunt

Come visit us...

www.creativeacademyforwriters.com

ACKNOWLEDGMENTS

There is nothing that I like more than the chance to practice my Nobel Prize in Literature speech. (You can picture me here talking into my hairbrush, likely wearing nothing fancier than a clean pair of yoga pants.)

First off, thank you for buying this book and giving me a chance to be a part of your writing journey. There are few things I enjoy more than talking about writing and craft, so I appreciate you spending your valuable time on this book. I hope you got a lot from it and that it helps to make your story better.

A huge thanks to everyone at The Creative Academy. (This is where I would hold up the Nobel Prize and say how this should go to all of you, when we all know there is no way you're getting that award out of my hot hands.) The Creative Academy is such a wonderful community of writers and creators. You all inspire me and push me to be a better writer.

In particular I want to think my beta crew who were early readers on this project. Who knew you guys were so anally retentive about commas? A call out to, Bonnie, Elissa, Jenny, Kirsten, Marie and Tracy. I deeply appreciate your attention to detail and suggestions on how to make this better.

To my series co-creators and writers, Crystal Hunt and Donna Barker. I could not have done this without you. In fact, you guys might have talked me into this project so I blame you for the late hours. Everything I work on with you is made by better by your input. Knowing I can count on your both is a huge gift to me.

I owe a debt to every writer, editor and agent I've met, who have shared their knowledge of this industry and helped to shape my own skills. A special call out to The Surrey International Writers Conference which was the first writing conference I ever attended and set the bar high for any to come after it. I've met so many good friends through that organization.

To my friends and family who stand by me both in my real life and when I'm playing with my imaginary friends. And lastly to my dogs who don't do anything useful but can be counted on for a laugh every so often.

ABOUT EILEEN COOK

Eileen Cook is a multi-published, award-winning author with her novels appearing in nine languages. Her books have been optioned for film and TV. She spent most of her teen years wishing she were someone else or somewhere else, which is great training for a writer. She's an instructor/mentor with The Creative Academy for Writers and Simon Fraser University's Writer's Studio program, where she loves helping other writers find their unique story to tell.

Eileen lives in Vancouver, Canada, with two very naughty dogs. You can learn more about her on her website at https://eileencook.com/ or connect with her on social media.

facebook.com/EileenCook.author
twitter.com/Eileenwriter
instagram.com/eileencookwriter

LIST OF RESOURCES

Do What You Are by Paul Tieger, Barbara Barron and Kelly Tieger, Little, Brown Spark, 2014

Emotional Intelligence by Daniel Goleman, Bantam Books, 2005

Emotional Thesaurus by Angela Ackerman and Becca Puglisi, JADD Publishing, 2018

GMC: Goal, Motivation and Conflict: The Building Blocks fo Good Fiction by Debra Dixon, Bell Bridge Books, 2013

Scrappy Rough Draft: Use science to strategically motivate yourself & finish writing your book by Donna Barker, The Creative Academy, 2019

Strategic Series Author: Plan, write and publish a series to maximize readership & income by Crystal Hunt, The Creative Academy, 2019

The Writer's Journey by Christopher Vogler, Michael Wise Productions, 2007

Writing the Breakout Novel: Insider Advice for Taking Your Fiction to the Next Level by Donald Maass, Writer's Digest Books, 2002

YOUR TURNS ALL IN ONE PLACE

Chapter Two

Exploring your own beliefs can be useful. Below is a checklist about people and their behaviours. Indicate true or false to each statement. There isn't a right or wrong answer to these questions (although feel free to debate it among your friends or family), rather it's part of your perspective on the world and how people move around in it. If you find yourself struggling with an answer remember that you are trying to answer it "more often than not" versus as an absolute, as there are always different situations and extenuating circumstances.

Then re-do the checklist below considering how your main character would answer those questions.

Visit our **https://creativeacademyforwriters.com/resources/buildbettercharacters/**page and download the **character belief sheet** as a printable worksheet.

True or False:

1. Most people in the world are generally good.
2. The world is random, there is no such thing as fate or destiny, things just happen.
3. Hard work is essential.
4. I'm anxious and worried about the future.
5. Common sense is not very common.
6. I have a balance of good and negative traits, but overall, I believe that I am special and unique in this world and have something to offer.
7. If someone is kind to you, they likely want something.
8. People can, and do, change.
9. It matters a lot to me what others think of me.
10. The way to move through life successfully is to make plans, evaluate options and then choose a direction.
11. I believe that things will generally work out for the best.
12. People will take advantage of you if they have an opportunity.
13. There is some kind of "purpose" to our lives, be it religion or the universe or the great spirit—there is some source of divine energy that looks out for us.
14. Everything happens for a reason. Even in bad times, there will be something for you to learn.
15. I put myself first.

16. People are who they are, they are unlikely to ever change.
17. Life should be lived in the moment. You have to react - people who try to plan everything are missing opportunities.
18. Family and friends are my most important priority.
19. I am not concerned with what other people think of me, it is more important that I approve of what I'm doing.
20. There is no such thing as a god, mystical power or caring universe. There is the world we have here, and what we do in it is all that matters.
21. I do not feel lucky, gifted or special.

Remember there is no right or wrong with the answers above. The quiz is designed to help you begin to understand your own perspective and feelings on yourself and how you interact with the world.

Chapter Three

- If your character is in physical danger, what is their most pressing safety concern? What scares them the most about this? How can you show that desperate need for survival?
- If your character is in a life or death situation, what might they do to survive that they wouldn't do in any other circumstance?
- If you have a situation that isn't life or death, does

it feel that way to the character? What do they think they will lose if they're not successful?

- Are there relationships missing in your character's life? Are their current relationships healthy?
- Have your character do a journal entry about love. What does it mean to them? Do they feel loved?
- What would make your character feel good about themselves?
- What would your character need to do to feel successful?
- What is your character's reputation? Do they like it, are they proud of it? What would they like their reputation to be?
- If all of your character's base needs have been met, what do they need to fully become their best self?
- Write a journal entry from the POV of one of your characters where they talk about their biggest dreams. If they could do anything/be anything, what would it be?

Chapter Five

Download the entire interview as a printable worksheet from **https://creativeacademyforwriters.com/resources/buildbettercharacters/.**

- Create a family tree/relationship tree or journal entry where your character talks about an early childhood memory.

- Your character's conflicts with their family members are a possible source of interesting backstory. What led up to this division? Is it something that should (or could) be healed over the course of the story, or is it a relationship best left separate?
- One way to think about a character's memories and their impact—is to think about your own, noticing what sticks out to you and what you might take from that in terms of how you view the world. In essence, I'm asking you to be your own counsellor.
- List the first memory of your own childhood that comes to mind and then 2-3 more.
- For each memory write out as much as you can recall about it. Sights, smells, sounds and what happened.
- Now how would you interpret this memory if you were a counsellor? Why do you think it stands out for you? What meaning might you put on to that memory? How has that situation/event impacted you later in life?
- Do you ever wonder if your memories are accurate? Do you have a childhood memory of an event or experience that a sibling has a *completely* different memory of?
- If your character has a different racial, cultural or religious background other than your own, what research have you done to get those details right?
- Can you identify anyone with a similar background who you could speak to?

- What is your character's current financial situation?
- Are they stressed about money?
- What types of resources do they have, or lack, as a result?
- Is your character married or in a long-term relationship? How would they describe that relationship?
- What is your character's relationship history? Are there any relationships that they regret?
- Is your character (happy / satisfied / unhappy) with their current relationship status?
- How would your character describe their social circle?
- Who is their "go to" person for when they are struggling?
- Is your character someone others rely on for support?
- If your character was asked about their relationship history, what would they say?
- How would your character's best friend describe them? Would this be different between a childhood best friend and someone who knows them in the present day?
- What is your character's religious background?
- Do they still believe in the faith they were raised in?
- Would others describe your character as spiritual?
- What does your character think happens to people after they die? Do they believe in heaven and hell?

- If their teachers were to fill out a form on your character what would they say? (i.e. Susan talks too much in class.) Do a report card for your character.
- If your character could take a class for fun, what would they take? Why?
- When your character thinks back on school, what memories stick out?
- What would your character's doctor say about them and their health?
- What ownership do they take for their health? Do they take the blame for something they can't control? (i.e. I got cancer because I'm somehow a bad person.)
- Consider how your character reacts to any health challenges. Do they under- or over-represent their abilities? Are there issues of secondary gain for them, and if so, what are they, and is the character aware of it?
- Do a resume for your character. With what they have done in the past, were they good at that role?
- What skills do they have?
- Who was your character's favourite boss (or least favourite)? Why?
- How long did they stay in various occupations and what were the reasons (perhaps real and what they admit to) for why they stayed or left?
- What was your character's favourite job? Least favourite? Why?

- Choose a few of the questions and interview your character. Or for a different twist, have someone else select questions and interview you where you respond from your character's POV. Record this so you don't have to pause and write down notes. Let the answers be spontaneous. You might be surprised at what you say.

Chapter Six

- Create a timeline for your character. The dot on the top is their birth. The dot on the bottom is the start of the story. What's happened to them? How do they view each life milestone?
- You can also create a timeline where the dot at the top is the start of your book and the dot at the bottom is the end of your story. Write down the major events that happen to your character in the plot, but also take note of how they view those events. Does the character list them to the right or left on the line?
- If you created a timeline, look through it. What have you learned about your character? What major events did they think to list? Are there any that they didn't list, but you as the author see as very important to who they are?
- You can also explore these events more fully. One way to do this is to write a journal entry from the character's POV (even if you're not using the first person to tell the story) the day or day after that event.

- Write a journal entry from the POV of another character who might share a memory of an event with your character. How do they see it? The same? Differently? What new perspective do they bring?
- Create timelines for your antagonist or other major characters in the story. How has what's happened to them impacted the choices and decisions they make in your story?

Chapter Fourteen

If you would like an easy way to answer these questions for your characters, download the **Character EQ Interview** from **https://creativeacademyforwriters.com/resources/buildbettercharacters.**

- On a scale of one to ten, where one is no awareness of their own emotions, and ten is highly aware of emotions, where does your character fall?
- Are there emotions that your character typically confuses with another emotion?
- If there are emotions that your character confuses, what is it about the emotion that they deny that triggers them? Do they have a value judgement about that emotion?
- Is there a story they tell themself that makes them unable to honestly acknowledge what they are feeling?
- When your character feels a strong emotion can they identify what caused it?

- On a scale of one to ten, where one means your character won't stand up for anything, and ten means that they are fully capable of standing up for themselves, where does your character fall?
- If your character doesn't stand up for themself, why? What do they tell themself when those things happen?
- Are there things that bother your character, that they won't stand up for?
- What are the things that make your character stand up? Is there a line that can't be crossed?
- On a scale of one to ten, where one means that your character has a horrible self-image (either completely negative or blindly positive) and ten means that they have a positive balanced self-image, where does your character fall?
- What does your character see as their strengths and weaknesses?
- What would other characters say about them? Have the other characters list ten words to describe your main character.
- How many of the descriptions are similar? Do different people in their life see your main character differently?
- Does your main character like themself? Why or why not?
- If your character doesn't like themself, do they talk negatively about themself or do they go the other way making up for insecurity by bragging?

- On a scale of one to ten, where one means that your character does not pursue anything beyond safety, and ten means that they have pursuits and interests that give meaning to their life, where does your character fall?
- What gives your character's life meaning?
- What is their passion?
- Are they following it? Why or why not?
- Do they believe people approve of their passion?
- Are their basic needs (survival, safety, healthy relationships) being met?
- If your book starts with the character having those basic needs met, and you are taking those away or putting them at risk due to events in your story, how does your character cope?
- On a scale of one to ten, where one means that your character feels incapable of making choices unless others provide a solution or approve of their decisions, and ten means that they're fully capable of making their own choices and seeks input only when and where they feel it will enhance their ability to make a good decision, where does your main character fall?
- Does your character trust their own decisions or do they look to others?
- If they look to others, whose opinion do they seek? Trusted friends or strangers?
- If they trust others to make decisions in their life, have they chosen wisely or do those people have other motivations which may not be in your character's best interest?

- Is your main character capable of pausing before making a choice?
- On a scale of one to ten, where one means that your character hasn't a clue what is happening inside others, and ten means that they are able to read and interpret others' emotions based on non-verbal cues, where does your character fall?
- Is your character "tuned in" to others?
- If they misread the situation, what do they assume?
- If your character is good at reading other's emotions, do they use this power for good, or do they manipulate it to get what they want?
- How does your character feel and respond when they realize that they completely missed how someone was feeling?
- How can your character's failure to recognize someone's subtext and non-verbal cues add conflict to your story?
- On a scale of one to ten, where one means that your character doesn't have any positive relationships (either that they're alone or that the relationships they do have are toxic), and ten means that they have a strong social support network of friends and family and works to ensure that these relationships remain healthy, where does your character fall?
- What relationships does your character have (family, friends, love)? Are these healthy relationships?

- If you were your character's best friend, what would you think of their relationships?
- How does your character interact with others when they are under stress? Do they lash out, or damage those relationships?
- Does your character believe they deserve good people in their life, or do they sabotage relationships because at some level they don't feel they are worthy?
- When your story heats up and the conflict is raised, what skills do other people in your character's life have that may help them?
- If there is someone in your character's life who is better suited to solve the problem, how can you remove that individual, so your protagonist must solve it themself? (This is why in so many YA (young adult) novels we kill off the parents. If the parents were healthy and helpful the main character would go to them.)
- Create a family tree for your character or a map of other social connections and friends.
- On a scale of one to ten, where one means that your character has no connections to their community that they would sacrifice for (or that they sacrifice far more than they should), and ten means that they have specific community connections where they are an active participating member (even though it may not always result in a direct benefit to them), where does your character fall?
- What causes are important to your character?

- Who, or for what will your character sacrifice their wishes and needs?
- What is your character risking by taking on this cause? Is there a way to increase those stakes?
- Does your character volunteer time or money to any causes?
- How far would your character go to help a group larger than themself?
- How do the people around your character feel about their sacrifices? Do they support the character or resent them?
- On a scale of one to ten, where one means that your character has horrid problem-solving abilities, and ten means that they are able to identify and respond to problems, where does your character fall?
- How does your character cope with problems? Would others describe them as a problem-solver?
- Do they even know that they have a problem? Or do they think things are out of their control?
- Are you sure the problem is something they can do something about? You want your character to have agency (the capacity to act).
- Unless you're writing a short story, your character likely won't solve the problem on the first try, or if they do solve that problem it creates a whole host of new problems. What happens if their first solution doesn't work? What new problems might come out of their actions?

- What is the impact of the attempted solutions on others in the story? You can increase conflict if your character's solution to a problem puts someone or something else they cherish, at risk.
- On a scale of one to ten, where one means that your character is unable to differentiate between reality and their personal experiences, and ten means that they understand the impact of their own filter on their perceptions of the world around them, where does your character fall?
- What does your character believe about the things that happen to them?
- Are their beliefs accurate?
- Is it their interpretation alone of what happened, or are others trying to manipulate the situation to have your character believe something that isn't true?
- How do they act based on their beliefs?
- If the same situation were to be seen by or happen to another character, what would that other character believe about the situation?
- Does your character have good insight into how their own filter impacts how they see the world, or do they think they're completely objective?
- On a scale of one to ten, where one means that your character can't flex at all no matter the situation, and ten means that they are able to flex their responses depending on their environment or the people around them, where does your character fall?
- How does your character deal with the unexpected or unfamiliar?

- How do they feel about change?
- If your character's approach to challenges no longer works, are they able to shift and try new solutions?
- Write a description of your character's ordinary world, what their life and routines look like before your story starts.
- On a scale of one to ten, where one means that your character falls apart under stress, and ten means that they respond to high-stress situations while remaining calm and focusing on what needs to be done, where does your character fall?
- How does your character cope with stress? What do they do when they are stressed?
- How does stress physically manifest itself in your character (headaches, tense shoulders, etc.)?
- How do they deal with situations where they are out of control?
- Prior to the book, what was the most stressful situation your character had dealt with?
- What situations does your character find stressful? For example, some people might cope well in high emergency situations like a fire, but fall apart if someone is emotionally upset.
- On a scale of one to ten, where one means that your character is unable to resist an impulse in any area, and ten means that they are able to control those impulses, weigh their decisions before acting and keep their eye on the long-term goal, not just the immediate payoff, where do your characters fall?
- How does your character respond when angry?

- Are there areas where your character struggles more with impulse control than another? For example, can they turn away from warm cookies, but are helpless when they see a sale on shoes?
- Are there particular emotional triggers that set your character off?
- What long-term goal would inspire your character to delay an impulse that they might otherwise give in to?
- Does your character respond the same way to an impulse when they are alone versus when others might see them?
- Most of us struggle more with impulse control in our teen years. This is how we end up in a range of bad situations. Write a journal entry where your character is looking back at a time in their youth when they had poor impulse control. What do they think of that event now? Do they think they would still act in the same way? Are they disappointed in themself?
- On a scale of one to ten, where one means that your character is unhappy most of the time and has extreme difficulty finding joy or seeing the bright side of things, and ten means that they know what makes them happy, are able see the positive or find humour even in dark situations, where does your character fall?
- What is fun for your character? What gives them joy?
- What things do they do (often these are small things, pausing for a cup of tea or a hot shower) that they know will pick up their mood?

- Would people describe them as happy? Why or why not?
- Do they rely on others to make them happy?
- When difficult or challenging things happen, do they find humour in it? Can they see the positive? If not, how do they respond when other people react that way?
- If your character is not happy, has this always been the case or did something happen that changed their outlook?
- On a scale of one to ten, where one means that your character is a complete pessimist who believes the world is a bad place and that there's no point in hoping for better, and ten means that they're an optimist even in difficult or challenging situations, where does your character fall?
- Does your character have a sense of hope about their future?
- What does your character feel about society and humanity? Do they see people as generally good and trustworthy?
- If your character's perspective on this scale has changed (either way), what led to that change?
- The book, *The Secret,* put forward a theory that if you put your hopes and desires out into the world, and if you ask for them, the universe will deliver. What would your character ask for, and would they believe that the universe will deliver?

- Many optimists believe in the power of positive thinking. One common element of this can be positive affirmations, things that we say to ourselves (often into a mirror) and repeat as a way to train our brain to believe them and to replace negative self-talk with this new positive perspective until the brain begins to believe it. Examples of positive affirmations include: I am smart and capable; I am strong, both physically and emotionally; I am a loveable person. What affirmations might your character be trying out? What negative thoughts would they be replacing?

Chapter Sixteen

Consider your character's attitude to interacting with the world. Would you classify them as an extrovert or an introvert? Some things to consider:

- After a long day, do they seek out social time with friends to unwind (extrovert) or prefer to go home with a glass of wine and Netflix (introvert)?
- Your character has a ton of hobbies that they dip in and out of (extrovert), or do they prefer to have one or two areas that they focus on (introvert)?
- Does your character have a wide range of friends, someone for every occasion (extrovert), or do they have a small band of friends (introvert)?
- Does your character find social events something that they can do at a moment's notice (extrovert), or do they feel like they have to "gear up" for a big night out (introvert)?

- Once you've decided if your main characters are extroverts or introverts score them on a scale of ten, one being not very strongly and ten being very strongly.
- If you want to increase internal conflict for your character, place them in a situation that pushes this scale. That is if they are extroverted, can you limit their interaction with others or have them be unable to act? If they're introverted how can you overload them with people? Consider forcing them to work closely with, or be in a relationship with, someone who is the exact opposite of them. They will almost certainly butt heads.
- Does your character like to approach problems by thinking about things in terms of data and what they know to be true and then weighing the options (sensing), or do they feel that their gut is a better way to decide (intuition)?
- When your character has a problem, do they back up and think about the big picture (intuition) or do they go about collecting objective data (sensing)?
- Once you've decided whether they lean toward sensing or intuition, score them on a scale of ten, one being not very strongly and ten being very strongly.
- Increase external conflict by having them interact with someone who approaches perception in a different way or increase internal conflict by having them doubt that the way they perceive information is working.

- When they need to make a decision, are they likely to weigh all the pros and cons (thinking,) or put an emphasis on how their decision will make other people feel (feeling)?
- Are they annoyed by people who seem illogical (thinking)?
- Is making everyone "buy in" important to them (feeling)?
- If they were buying a car, would your character research all the *Consumer Reports* and ratings (thinking) or would they try a range of cars and see what gives them the best feeling once they sit in it (feeling)?
- Once you've decided if they are thinking or feeling, score them on a scale of ten, one being not very strongly, and ten being very strongly.
- There are likely many opportunities to increase conflict around decision-making points in your book. Can you maximize any of these by contrasting your character's style with those around them or having their preferred approach not work for them in a particular situation?
- When planning a trip is your character the type to plan everything and research what they want to see before they go (judging) or do they prefer to just arrive and see what happens (perceiving)?
- If your character is going to join a table at a party would they choose people they know or are certain are similar to them (judging) or would they prefer to just plop down and start talking to new people (perceiving)?
- If going to university, would your character think

through schedules, career opportunities and potential earnings before choosing a major (judging) or would they take courses in areas that interest them and decide later what to focus on (perceiving)?

- Once you've decided if they are judging or perceiving, score them on a scale of ten, one being not very strongly and ten being very strongly.
- Look through your manuscript. Are there opportunities to increase conflict by having the character interact with someone who has the opposite approach to them?
- Consider your character's backstory. How did those events shape which preferences they have on the different scales?
- Will your character's MBTI score be the same at the end of your book?
- The results of the MBTI are sixteen different personality profiles. If you've done the exercises above, you have a pretty good idea of what your character's type is.
- Make a list of the MBTI codes for each of your main characters. Write out their description and consider how well they will work together. Where will they buttress each other's strengths and weaknesses? Where will conflict likely arise?
- If you are writing a series, you'll need to consider how characters change and evolve over several books. To assist you in developing a system to track series details including characters and character details consult Crystal Hunt's book

Strategic Series Author: Plan, write and publish a series to maximize readership & income.

Chapter Eighteen

What change is your character resisting? Brainstorm three push reasons and three pull reasons. Use one, or all, to help them through this process.

Chapter Nineteen

- What is an example of a significant change you needed to make in your life? Write a journal entry about that change. What made you want to make it? What were some of the competing interests that kept you from making that change? What kept you going when things got difficult?
- Look at your character's current situation. What would further motivate them to pursue their goal? Asking the question, *What would make this worse?* is a great way to increase the conflict.
- Look at the goal the character is trying to reach, what would make obtaining that goal even more meaningful for them? How can you make the goal more desirable, and thus irresistible to the character even though you are going to make it difficult for them to obtain? How can it matter *more* if they achieve that goal?

Chapter Twenty

- Watch the film adaptation of a book you've read. (Yes, I know the book was better.) Look at how the screenwriter adapted the work. What approach did they use to show the character change?
- Take a few scenes from your book that have a lot of internal dialogue. Challenge yourself to come up with a list of ways that you could show the character doing something that would illustrate what they were thinking about a change.

Chapter Twenty-one

- What change does your character need to make over the course of the story?
- How will this change impact how they see the world, see others, and themself?
- How many sitting and talking (S&T) scenes do you have in your book? Is there a way to put those characters into action instead? They might still have some of the same dialogue, but how can the action enhance the scene?

Chapter Twenty-two

- If your character is at a pre-contemplation stage, what story or narrative do they tell themself that makes them downplay or ignore the problem?
- Are there other characters in your manuscript who

recognize there is a problem? How have they tried to raise this issue with your character? How did this go over?

- What excuses does your character have for not changing at this time?
- What are the pros of the character staying in their current life without making a change?
- What are the cons of the character making a change?
- In your manuscript what kinds of resources or information does your character need to make a plan? Where will they go to find these things?
- What things can you place into the setting and surroundings that your character could begin to notice?
- Is there a character in your story who can serve in the mentorship role and help your protagonist? And keep in mind if you have a wiser, more capable mentor character you're going to have to create a reason that this mentor can't solve the problem themselves. Your inner serial killer strikes yet again.
- Does your character have any kind of ritual to mark the fact they are embarking on a change? Examples might be a makeover, new clothing, holding some kind of ceremony, telling others, cleaning the house, destroying something that symbolizes what they are changing, etc.
- What are the positive experiences that your character has at the start of a new change?

- As the change continues, what are the challenges that the character faces that make them wonder why in the world they thought this decision was a good idea?
- How do the people around them respond to this change? Are they supportive?
- What are the things that your character needs to do to show they are continuing to make a positive change?
- What internal challenges will your character face when making a change?
- What external challenges will your character face when making a change?
- Will your character "relapse" into past behaviour? What is the final thing that pushes them over into this?
- How does your character react when they relapse into old behaviours?
- How do people around them react when your character relapses?
- What makes your character finally triumph?

Chapter Twenty-three

- What people or events around your character make them aware that they have a problem?
- Is there another character in the story who can be an example to your protagonist about what will happen to them if they do (or don't) change?
- What strong emotion is most difficult for your character to handle?

- Is there someone who has the most impact on them (a child, best friend, parent) whose opinion would garner a strong emotional reaction?
- Look around your character's space, what does that space say about them? If you're wanting to show that they're making a change, what about their space changes?
- Now do the same with what they're wearing. What clothing does your character wear and what does their style say about them? Are they happy with what they're communicating, or would they wear something different if they felt confident to do so?
- If your character was to have a dream about the life they would like to have, what would it look like?
- Is there someone around your character who could assist them in imagining their life in a new way?
- What options does your character have when making a change?
- Write down negative things that your characters say about themselves. How could they start to spin these toward the positive?
- What carrots would be meaningful for your characters to motivate them to keep going?
- What sticks would be meaningful for your characters to get them motivated?
- Are these sticks or carrots coming from inside your characters (as a result of self-reflection and evaluation), or are they coming from an external source?

- What change(s) does your character need to make over the course of the story? Distill this down to no more than three sentences.
- If the change is internal, how do you plan to show this externally? That is, if they need to learn to trust others, what will this look like? What will they say or do that shows the outside world that they are trusting?
- What do the people around your character think of this change? Are they supportive or do they sabotage your character? What does their support look like? If they aren't helpful, what are they doing and why are they doing it?
- What motivates your character to make this change? What motivates them not to change? They will likely have motivations on both sides, remember they want to write a book, but they also want to binge-watch that new show.
- How does your character's physical space reflect their internal status? Does this change over the course of the book?
- What does your character gain from a change? How would their life be better?
- What does your character give up if they make this change?
- Does your character fail in their effort to make the change?

- How does your character respond to the failure? Do they have a system of rewards or punishments to keep them going? If you have a moment in the book when it seems like all is lost and the character is teetering on the brink of giving up, what gives them hope to try one more time?
- How do others around your character respond to failure?

Made in the USA
Las Vegas, NV
24 May 2021